Author (or Heading)   MCINTYRE, J.

Title   Vol. No.
The shape of Christology.

Shelf Mark

THEOLOGY BT 202.M182

Please return this book as soon as you have finished with it.   All
books must be returned by the date shown below or when recalled
for another reader.

DATE DUE BACK

THE SHAPE OF CHRISTOLOGY

THE SHAPE OF CHRISTOLOGY

JOHN McINTYRE

*The Annie Kinkead Warfield Lectures
of 1965 delivered in
Princeton Theological Seminary*

SCM PRESS LTD
BLOOMSBURY STREET LONDON

FIRST PUBLISHED 1966
© SCM PRESS LTD 1966
PRINTED IN GREAT BRITAIN BY
ROBERT CUNNINGHAM AND SONS LTD
ALVA, SCOTLAND

CONTENTS

PREFACE

It was a wise Providence which inspired Dr Warfield to insert in the terms of the Annie Kinkead Warfield Lectureship an instruction that 'every Lecturer shall publish the Lectures within twelve months after their delivery'. Indeed, the proverbial slip 'twixt the cup and the lip is as nothing compared with that between lectures and publication. So the Warfield Lecturer cannot but be grateful that even though grace abounds, the law nevertheless compels. The text published here formed the substantial basis of the Lectures as actually delivered in February 1965.

The invitation to deliver the Annie Kinkead Warfield Lectures is in itself honour sufficient, but the event surpasses even the expectation. I should like, therefore, to place on record my very sincere appreciation of the generous welcome extended to me by President and Mrs G. I. McCord and by Professor G. S. Hendry of Princeton Theological Seminary, and of the warmth of the hospitality shown to me by Professor and Mrs James Barr in their own home. It would be ungracious of me not to mention also the stimulus provided by the attendance and attention of the audience in the Miller Chapel, and by the questions of the students in discussion thereafter.

New College
University of Edinburgh
Whitsuntide 1965

I

WHAT IS GIVEN IN CHRISTOLOGY

SYNOPSIS

Christocentricism is one of the distinctive characteristics of contemporary systematic theology. Christocentricism has two forms of expression: first, *all* doctrines are presented in christological context; secondly, christology provides a basic interpretative structure for the explication of other areas of doctrine.

The shape of any discipline is a function of three variables: the given upon which the discipline operates; the models which it employs for the systematization, exposition, analysis and interpretation of this given; and thirdly the method followed in operating the models.

We begin by examining the notion of the given generally. Several accounts of it are possible:

1. That which is given to the percipient; it is an immediate deliverance of some external situation.
2. The premises for a deduction (Euclid).
3. The problematical (N. Kemp Smith).
4. The content of experience attributable to external stimulus.
5. The total situation.
6. Subject-matter, what a discipline is all about.

The same given may serve a variety of purposes. Example of painting by Albert Namatjira.

The given of Christology:

1. Holy Scripture. Problem of this view. *Testimonium internum.*
2. Basic factual historical data.
3. God's self-revelation.
4. The here-and-now self-presentation to men of Jesus Christ.
5. The given of christology is a complex structure which involves all of the previous elements; as well as the confessional or credal tradition of our denomination; and the response of the believing community.

What is given in Christology

IF WE were asked to give in a summary form *the* distinguishing characteristic of Protestant theology in our time, many of us would reply that it is its christocentric quality which claims this title. And the evidence would be convincing. It could be shown that not since the days of Marcion has there been such an exclusive emphasis upon the absolute significance of Jesus Christ, not indeed in the whole history of Christian doctrine has there been any attempt such as we have seen in our day to locate revelation only in the person of Jesus Christ and to deny its occurrence elsewhere in God's creation. Ours is the period of theology which invented the phrase 'Christ, the centre of history' and interpreted historical process as a span between his first and his second coming, so that all events contained therein derived their significance from this twofold reference. It is an emphasis which has appeared also in the more strictly biblical disciplines—in the contentions that Christ stands between the Old Testament and the New, as the person to whom the one points forward and the other points back; or that Christ is the unity of the Old and New Testaments; or again that the two Testaments are 'all about Christ' and that typological exegesis is the only proper method for the right presentation of the biblical message.

Two forms of christocentricism

In the doctrinal field, christocentricism has come to have two meanings. First, it may be applied to a process in which doctrines are presented, not *seriatim* like pegs on a line only externally related to one another, but by being severally related to the doctrine of the person of Jesus Christ. For example, the doctrine of creation, which on the *seriatim* method of doctrinal presentation would come at the beginning of systematics and thereafter be forgotten about, on a christocentric presentation is at once related to God's redemptive purpose in Christ; creation is in order to redemption; the first creation is fulfilled in the new

9

creation. The covenant with Israel is the prototype and promise of the covenant which will be fulfilled in the broken bread and the wine poured forth. If the fulfilment cannot be understood apart from the promise, *a fortiori* the promise is empty without the fulfilment. So too, with eschatology; it is no longer taken solely as the final stage in the economy of redemption, the ultimate consummation in the end-time of the whole process: it has been integrated with christology and now it stands at the centre of the interpretation of Christ, and it adds a new dimension to the scale of the understanding of the person of Christ. Christology, in other words, becomes the medium of theological integration and of its intensional complexity.

Christocentricism has, however, taken a second form in modern theology, namely, that of providing a basic interpretative structure for the explication of other areas of doctrinal material. In the two natures and one person of the Chalcedonian Christ is discerned an analogical formula which can be employed in areas of theology that are not immediately recognizable as christological. For example, it is not uncommon to interpret the unity of divine and human in the Church or in the Bible, or in the sacraments, in a manner determined by the co-existence of human and divine in Jesus Christ. Of course, this application has to be strictly analogical and not univocal, or at once heresies would arise in the interpretative process. But the mention of heresy—and heresy is never very far away when the Chalcedonian definition is under consideration—draws our attention to a further noteworthy feature of the christocentricism of modern theology, namely, that it provides a working criterion of theological truth. In other words, christocentricism is not merely a medium of theological expression in our time; it is a norm of theological validity. It has been largely pressed into this office, as we shall see later, because of the failure of so many of the norms which have operated with such cogency in the past. Such norms as the Holy Scriptures themselves, the confessions of our churches (the classical creeds or the Westminster Confession), or even 'the inner testimony of the Holy Spirit', have all for one reason or another proved unable to operate as a single unambiguous criterion by which a point of doctrine could be settled with utter finality.

New functions of christology

It is by this time clear, then, that christology has come to exercise in theology a range of functions for some of which it was not originally designed: in this range we find exegetical, expository and hermeneutical as well as normative and critical elements. At this point two sets of questions inevitably arise. First, to what extent can the old christology forged in the controversies of the fourth and fifth centuries and re-expressed in the sixteenth, sustain the weight of responsibility placed upon it in this new and varied context? In other words, have the many changes both within theology and in the cultures within which Christian theology has been from time to time formulated in any way affected the adequacy of the classical christology to the tasks which it has been set? Secondly, to what extent have these new tasks altered the character of the classical christology itself? Has it remained a constant in the variety of functions to which it has been adapted? It will be my main contention that classical christology has come under severe strain in these new settings in which it has of late found itself and that a crisis has begun to develop which can only be resolved by a radical reassessment of the basic *shape* of this central doctrine of the Christian faith as today expressed. These questions which I have been raising are so closely related to the basic structures of christology that no attempt to answer them can easily escape the more radical analysis.

The given

The *shape* of any discipline may be regarded as a function of at least three variables: the given upon which the discipline operates; the models which it employs in the systematization, organization, exposition, analysis, interpretation and, in some cases, even the defence, of this given; and, thirdly, the method followed in operating these models. All three of these variables coalesce in the determination of the shape of christology, as they do of any other discipline; and our first task is to examine the first of these variables, namely, the given. Perhaps it may be of value partly to throw light upon the christological usage, partly to point out the contrast between the christological and the ordinary usage, to bring out the different elements involved in the ordinary notion of the given. What we are not prepared for, perhaps, is the variety of content which the ordinary usage has, and which is a partial explanation of the complexity of the christological uses. The various meanings of the given are as follows:

The given as immediate deliverance

First, the given may mean exactly what it says: it is that which is given directly to the percipient, or the knower. Here several points are being made. For example, the method of knowing is direct intuition of one kind or another. The given is the immediate deliverance of some external situation, which is immediately intuited. The percipient or the knower is not thought of as himself contributing anything to the given; indeed, any such contribution would at once introduce the possibility of falsification or misrepresentation. It would certainly reduce the purity of the given. In this sense, then, the given has a kind of intrinsic self-evidence; it carries its authority with it; it is thought to impose itself on the human mind from the outside. It is contrasted with interpretation, which is a conceptualization of its simplicity. The given also has or is thought to have the quality of immunity to being doubted. In itself, it is unquestionable in a manner denied to the conclusions which we draw from it or the interpretations we impose upon it. It is regarded, consequently, as having a degree of universality which is denied to the latter additions to it; it is acknowledged by all who care to inspect the situation which it constitutes. The given, in this form, becomes a court of appeal, something to be cited in order to clinch an argument, something compelling, something immediately inspectible and readily accessible.

The given as logical point of departure

Secondly, a more precise form of the first meaning of the given is to be derived from Euclidean geometry. There the given is the premises from which the conclusion is to be logically deduced. In proceeding to the conclusion we do not add anything by way of private interpretation to what is already stated in the given, or implicit in it. The latter qualification has to be made, because the entire axioms and postulates of Euclidean geometry are not enunciated every time the given of any theorem or proposition to be proved is stated. But they are, as it were, contained within the given as conditioning its very statement. In proceeding deductively to the conclusion, the *Q.E.D.* which every schoolboy knows, we are moving within the framework of an aprioristic conceptual system. While recognizing that there are other, and contradictory, accounts of what is involved in deductive reasoning, I am not at the moment concerned with them; for there are enough people who take the presently expounded account of the given to justify our nominating it as one of the accepted accounts of what is meant by this complex term. A distinction is here being drawn which will be seen to be of importance in the christological context between the given as the basis of interpretations which may variously be imposed upon it (our first sense) and the given as the starting-point of a demonstration within a conceptual system (our second sense), a demonstration which follows by strict logical steps from the given as the premises. On the first sense, the given contains only what is immediately inspectible; on the second, it is rather like an iceberg with its major fraction submerged, and accessible only by dint of deep, submarine probing.

The given as the problematical

Thirdly, there is a view of the given, first expounded to me by my old teacher, Professor N. Kemp Smith, which regards it not as the crystal clear premise of an argument or deduction which can be drawn from it, but as a situation which in itself is essentially problematical. In terms of our first sense of the given it may be immediately inspectible—as an event in the sense-perceptible world, as a sensory experience more closely related to our bodies, as an emotional disturbance, or as a reading on an instrument. It may be open to public and universal examination, and it may force itself upon us with a certain undeniable objectivity. But for Kemp Smith none of these qualities of the given would constitute its *differentia*, which would be its capacity to present itself to us as a situation which was not self-explanatory, or self-authenticating—as a situation which was essentially a problem requiring some solution. The given would have this quality primarily because it was not immediately to be explained in terms of the information that we already had at our disposal; in fact, it might seem at some points to contradict established knowledge and to call it in question.

Understanding the given in this way, Kemp Smith saw it as the springboard of all genuine advance in knowledge—ranging from the simplest visual problem created by the appearance of the station to move as we sit apparently at rest in the train, to the complex enigmas created for the scientist by the odd behaviour of the denizens of the microscopic world. So far from lulling us into any sense of security by its self-assurance and precision of definition, the given creates a world of difficulties for us; it may even occasion despair and deep confusion of mind; it is not a blinding light or the final clarity. But it *is* creative—creative of that process which is only finally successful when the problem of the given is solved in a wider context of comprehensibility. One point is particularly noteworthy, namely, that a certain amount of perceptiveness is required in order to know when the given is problematical. It must be *seen* to be contradicting established principles and laws before it acquires the character of the problematical. It has to be seen to have a certain oddness before it sets genuine problems, which once set leave no peace short of their solution. Men had been observing apples falling from the beginning of time, on one occasion at least to their sorrow, but it was the perceptiveness of Newton which discerned the problem within the given and which finally compelled the problem to yield its solution, or at least its adequate description, if solution be no longer the permissible word in this connection. In a very real sense then, it is the problematical quality of the given which constitutes it as the given, because it singles it out from what has been called 'the manifold of sense', or 'the big, buzzing, blooming confusion', for precise and particular observation, analysis, description and solution.

A further respect in which this third sense of the given differs from the previous two is that whereas on their rendering the given remains unaltered throughout the subsequent process of interpretation or deduction, in a very real way the sheet-anchor of the whole process, on this rendering, the given does alter character as the problem it sets is gradually solved; it acquires depth, richness of context, fuller meaning, as we would say. In a rather interesting way the authoritative quality which attached to the given in sense one above reappears in sense three in a normative quality which it now evinces: *it* is the problem which any solutions must solve. If any aspect of the given has been misrepresented, distorted or omitted, then the solution is to be discounted. If, therefore, the given is the starting-point of the enquiry, it is also the point of final return, for any explanation of the given stands or falls by what it makes of the problems set by the given.

The given as the externally originated

Fourthly, there is another way of looking at the given—much less romantic and highfalutin; one which regards the given as an abstract, something rather artificially excerpted from a very complex totality, and quite falsely regarded as capable of self-existence. Clearly there is implied here, as indeed in all three previous senses, an epistemological theory, namely, that what we know is an amalgam of external stimulus and categorical conceptualization. The given is thus equated with the content of consciousness attributable to external stimulus; but in the nature of the case it is not able to have any existence apart from the total cognitive situation, or if it does have such an existence, it has it in a totally different form; there can be no such thing as an unsensed sensum, or an unperceived perception. Sense four may be distinguished from sense one by the fact that while in sense one the given as in sense four comes from beyond the knowing or experiencing subject, in sense one the given has independence of existence, ultimacy and authority whereas in sense four it has none of these attributes. This difference is largely due to the fact that sense one reflects a naive realistic epistemological theory which is often rather innocently carried over into theological epistemology, as we shall see, with rather unfortunate consequences.

The given as privately apprehended

Fifthly, the instability of the given as defined in sense four induces me to propose a modification of this sense, according to which the given would be the total situation, what is imposed upon the knowing or perceiving mind from the outside plus the categorial conceptualization or any other interpretation present at the start. This sense is a much less sophisticated form of the term than that presented by Kemp Smith. As I have said it does not carry any of the elaborate qualities assigned to the given in senses one and two; but it does have the merit of drawing attention to one or two important considerations. For example, as against sense one, it recognizes that what is given for one person may differ from what is given for another, even though there is sufficient material common to the two 'givens' to justify their being taken for the same situation. It does also draw attention to the fact that the given from which we start in any discipline is an extremely complex situation which is a combination of private and public, subjective and objective, externally imposed and personally interpreted circumstances. Even in an apparently abstract, aprioristic discipline, where the axioms and postulates, the theorems and the propositions have apparently highly rational and objective character, they nevertheless reflect quite private and personal systems of preference and selection.

The given as the subject-matter of a discipline

So sixthly, we might say that the given of any discipline is its subject-matter—what it is all about. This sense would include sense five but relate it to a discipline—making it the content of the discipline as well as its starting-point, making it the central subject of the discipline as well as its initiating circumstances. In this sense are gathered up most of the other things which we have been saying about the given; for the subject-matter of any discipline is basically something imposed upon us and not of our own arbitrary devising; it is, too, the premises from which all our investigations flow; with its problems and enigmas it stimulates and sustains our curiosity and concern; and it forms the contextual framework within which the whole discipline operates.

Attitudes to the given

Certain points may now be summarized from the review of the use of the idea of the given in certain intellectual disciplines.

To begin with, we can see that the term applies to a considerable variety of content, some interpreters preferring to limit it to a fairly narrow, sophisticated minimum, others regarding it as a fairly comprehensive if somewhat unsystematized starting-point of the discipline. One of the major tasks, therefore, confronting any discipline is to define the range and content of its given. Another important point emerging from this preliminary discussion is that correlative to the interpretation of the given is a certain attitude on the part of the practitioner. Very often the given specifies the attitude to be taken up to it, but it is also permissible, as we shall see, to adopt a variety of attitudes to the given even where it is interpreted in one single way. The cases of a one-one correlation between the given and the appropriate attitude are fairly obvious. Where the given is interpreted as self-authenticating, then its presentation to the observer is compulsive; his proper attitude is receptivity and acknowledgment. If, on the other hand, the given comes in the form of the problematical, then a blind acceptance of its self-presentation would yield only confusion. The correct attitude here is to question, to analyse, to probe, to wonder. Where the given is the clearly enunciated premises of a deduction to be drawn from them, then the application of strict logical thinking to this process is what the situation demands.

We are, therefore, in fact now taking a further step and saying that the given not only determines the appropriate attitude to adopt towards it; it also prescribes the method we must follow in its explication. It should be added that such prescription may take the form of permitting several possibilities, while at the same time eliminating certain others. There is not always a necessary correlation between one interpretation of the given and one certain attitude.

The given, moreover, may be used to serve a variety of ends, and it will be such ends which determine which of the methods permitted by the given is employed in the event. For example, let us take as our given a system of visual sense-data which would be identified at Sotheby's, London, as a painting by the late Albert Namatjira, a member of the Arunta tribe in Australia. This given in the context for which it was designed, becomes the subject of aesthetic pleasure, and this attitude will determine the method we shall follow in further examining and describing it. But this same given may happen to be in the room where the Aristotelian Society is having its meetings, and the picture, now treated strictly as a collection of visual sense-data, features as such as an illustration of the term 'sense-data' in a series of arguments. In this context, it is entertained in a rather different attitude; and the method of dealing with it is vastly different from that of aesthetic appreciation. It is the method of analysis and investigation, of perceptual consideration and even of pure sensing. Again, because Namatjira is reputed to have made his own pigments by an expert use of some of the soils in central Australia, the colours in the picture may serve a geological or an agricultural purpose. The paints throughout may be submitted to chemical analysis and the colours in this context may be of great significance. The geological end determines quite clearly the method which the analyst follows in treating the samples of soil appearing in the picture. A psychiatrist, whose interest lies in a correlation between mental attitudes and artistic production, may detect in Namatjira's depiction of the loneliness of 'the dead heart of Australia' something of the social, religious and cultural vacuum which the advent of western culture and Christianity has created for the native peoples of Australia. Finally, a photographer who has come to despair over the inability of the various commercial companies to produce a complete spectrum of reliable colour-reproductions—the companies that are good with the greens turn out a red that looks orange—might well see in Namatjira's colour system the faithfulness of total reproduction which seems still to baffle the efforts of modern photographic science.

To summarize the conclusions to be drawn from this illustration, we may say that the term, the given, may apply to a variety of content even in respect of the same situation; that the same single given appearing in a variety of contexts or subserving a variety of ends may allow of a variety of attitudes to be adopted to it; and finally, there is a close, though not always a one-one, correlation between the view taken of the given and the method employed in exploring it, and a uniformly close correlation between the attitude taken to the given and the method employed in exploring it.

The given in christology

In turning now to the given of christology, we may at once anticipate certain complicating circumstances which will prevent us from simply 'reading off' the characteristics of an immediately and directly intuitable situation. First, there is the combined force of the considerations which we have just presented, namely, that the very notion of the given is itself non-simple. It is no refutation of this point to argue that the theological image converts the non-simplicity of the secular content into transparent clarity, for in fact there is a carry-over, as we shall see, of the non-simplicity into the theological reference. Secondly, when we look specifically at the theological situation, we find that there are several candidates for the office of the given and that as a result one of the main tasks is to judge among their several claims or alternatively to discover how indeed they may be reconciled with one another. I can conceive of no more urgent task in contemporary theology, for the recognition of the claim of any situation to be the given at once invests it with an authority, an ultimacy, and a status which compels the obeisance of the other members of the theological firmament. Indeed I am inclined to think that most of our theological disagreements are ultimately disagreements about the given. Thirdly, it is noteworthy that there is a problem not only concerning the candidates for the office of the given, but also as to what the content of the given is, once one of the candidates has his/its claims recognized. This question is not simply a repetition of the second, because people who agree, say, that Christ is the given of christology, might radically disagree over the content to be assigned to this given. Fourthly, we shall expect the discussion of the given of christology to be incomplete without some examination of the methods to be followed according to the different conceptions of the given.

Scripture as the given

Perhaps the most obvious candidate for the office of the given in christology is holy scripture, particularly the New Testament. There is no doubt that in the classical formative periods of christology, it was the scriptures which constituted the given—

not simply for the orthodox whose formulae triumphed, but also for the heretics who contended to the last that orthodoxy was a misrepresentation of the given of scripture. It is also true that in modern christological controversies it is common practice to quote scripture as a final court of appeal as if it constituted a given common to all sides of the controversies. There is, therefore, an almost immediately convincing case for affirming that scripture is the given of christology, given in the sense of being literally and authoritatively definitive of all that is affirmed within christology; and that we ought forthwith to desist from further search. But the matter is not so easy as that—for a number of reasons.

First, it is doubtful whether anyone operates with the *whole* of scripture as his given, so that this form of the given as authoritative would be valid only for someone who was a completely consistent fundamentalist. As soon as we allow any principle of selection to operate, and there are few people who do not, then we have departed from allegiance to the total given-ness and the single prescriptiveness of scripture. On this ground, it is not to be assumed that scripture may not turn out to be the given in some other sense already defined.

Secondly, it has always been an essential part of the Reformed view of scripture that its true meaning is only rightly discerned through the *testimonium internum spiritus sancti*. Whatever else this fairly complex doctrine may mean, it does at least imply that the meaning of scripture cannot be simply 'read off', as one would rightly expect it to be were one dealing with an immediately intuitable and authoritative given. Thirdly, it is very doubtful whether any one of us can now read scripture except through the medium of the numerous interpretative symbols which the Church has constructed to ensure our right understanding of scripture. The function of the confessions formulated by the Reformers has not always been fully appreciated in this connection. The Confessions have been, of course, correctly regarded as short summaries of the faith to be used as a basis for instructing the young and confuting heretics or unbelievers. But they also had initially a further purpose, namely, that of providing the interpretative structure for the right understanding of scripture. It is here that our present lack of confessional clarity is proving to be most harmful, in that it deprives our contemporaries, and particularly those who have to teach the young, of the adequate means of catechetical interpretation of scripture. If, then, we wish to persist with the view that the scripture is the given, then we have in honesty also to acknowledge that it is a given which comes to us in an extremely confused mixture of credal, confessional and modern theological additions.

Fourthly, the researches of New Testament scholars have shown that the scriptures bear many signs themselves of being interpretative, and that it is possible by judicious and careful comparison and criticism to uncover some passages among those immediately delivered by scripture that are more original than others. Another way of stating this same matter takes a theological form: scripture is not the given itself; it is the witness to the given. We shall later examine the claims of this something standing behind scripture to be the given of christology, but at the moment we may simply note that in a sense scripture is not self-contained or self-complete, and that in fact on its own confession it derives its authority from beyond itself. It cannot therefore be the given in the sense that it is ultimate or self-authenticating.

Fifthly, such a conclusion, however, does leave open the possibility that scripture may still be the given of christology in that it constitutes both its starting-point and its finishing-point: it prescribes the problems and defines the issues with which a fully articulated and integrated christology must finally deal. Such is the position for which I intend finally to argue but in the meantime it is necessary to examine the claims of other candidates.

Minimal historical core as the given of christology

Dissatisfaction with the view that scripture is the given of christology has led to departures in two directions. The first, following the acknowledgment that scripture is itself an interpretation of certain prior historical events, leads to the contention that the given for christology is those basic uninterpreted events which would be accepted by an agnostic scientific historian as having happened. Christology is then presented as an elaboration of these basic data agreed upon by everyone: the agnostic differs from the Christian in his refusal to make what he believes to be an otiose interpretation. *Entia non multiplicanda praeter necessitatem.* Christians differ from one another in the range they give to their interpretations.

This view has a certain *a priori* attractiveness and strength in that it resembles the epistemological theory which regards sense-data as the given of the perceptual situation, in which they are elaborated into physical objects. But the attractiveness ends there. For it inherits all the fallacies of that epistemological theory, and particularly its failure to realize that such apparently simple entities as sense-data or uninterpreted historical events are arrived at only after a great deal of very sophisticated conceptual thought. They never exist for anyone at any time as the simply given in any of our previously nominated senses. In fact, in order to exist at all they have to be embodied in situations in which interpretation has already taken place. In the case of christology, it is impossible even to describe the so-called uninterpreted given, the single common observable for unbeliever and believer alike; for any description involves immediate interpretation of one kind or another. This so-called given of christology has to be rejected as an abstraction, or a will o' the wisp, one which nevertheless was pursued by many exponents of the historical Jesus school. But many who have no longer any sympathy with that school retain the idea that some such abstraction constitutes the basic core of the factuality or the historicity of Jesus' life and death, a core which might somehow be reached through the removal of successive layers of interpretation and elaboration. If, in fact, it did prove possible conceptually to reach some such minimal historical core, it would be quite wrong to characterize it as the given in any sense.

The given as God's self-revelation in Jesus Christ

A further departure from dissatisfaction with the view that scripture itself is the given of christology is made in the direction of saying that the given is God's self-revelation in Jesus Christ. The Bible points beyond itself to the self-revelation of God, which thus imposes itself upon the believer. It requires no authority outside of itself to establish its credentials; it bears the marks of its own authenticity, and so commends itself to the believer that he is left without occasion for question or doubt. To be exposed to this reality to which the Bible witnesses is to be convinced by it. This self-revelation is the ultimate; it is normative of all else that is to be said about God. It demands a single attitude from us of obedience and worship; in this context anything else would be blasphemy or unbelief. It is immediately intuited and does not involve any interpretative process on the human side. That precisely is the reason for the prominence which such a view is given today in most conservative groups in modern theology—that it rejects the whole natural theological movement according to which God may be known by some process of argument from the created world, or from man's moral nature. God is known only in Jesus Christ and only be-cause he comes to us from the other side of the infinite gulf that separates the Creator from the creature. The emphasis is a sound one and one which had to be made, but it is difficult to resist the question of whether it constitutes a finally valid an-swer to the question of the given of christology. In other words, it may be a perfectly valid answer to a question, but not to *this* question. Let me try to indicate what I mean.

The contention that in christology we have to deal with a subject-matter which is not the finest and ultimate flowering of human inventiveness is a perfectly permissible way of saying that at the core of christology there is an event, there is a person who comes from right outside of the human situation as we know it. This intrusion, this intervention cannot be reduced to some psychological compensation or to a hallucinatory status. Thus stated, this view can be clearly seen to be an anti-state-ment, a rejection of that form of liberalism which was prepared to have 'religion without revelation'. But its virtues as an anti-statement do not serve it well where positive issues are to be solved. What is contained in this given which is God's self-revelation? The short answer, one might say the conventional answer, is: God himself; but the unsatisfactoriness of this solu-tion may be based on the following considerations. To begin with, it is obvious that the short answer at once raises the further questions of the nature, attributes and characteristics both of the person in whom the revelation is taking place and of the

23

person who is there revealed. When these questions are in their turn answered, then many of the traditional biblico-theological, or credal or doctrinal formulae are produced. In present-day conservative theology, it is the Chalcedonian christological pattern which is presented as the form of the divine revelatory event. Now if it really is intended from the start that the given of christology is the traditional Chalcedonian picture of Jesus Christ and of the God who is his father, then perhaps this fact ought to be stated from the start, and not introduced half-way through the discussion under the guise of revelation to reinforce a position or an interpretation which can historically be shown to have other sources.

We shall later be returning to a fuller examination of the place of the idea of revelation in christology but at the moment we may make these further brief comments. The idea of revelation does not of itself add any *content* to the given of christology. It is an account of how we come by this given, or more correctly, of how this given comes to us. But of itself it may permit quite a wide range of doctrinal variation. For example, Barth and Brunner both use the idea extensively in their christological assertions, yet they also differ quite extensively. A defence of the position we have been examining might be made by pointing out that in the revelatory process the believer is directed beyond or through the medium of revelation to that which is being revealed. It is then a case of immediate knowledge of an independently existing and specifically characterized reality. Without considering whether it is right to regard Christ as a medium beyond or through whom we must pass in knowing God through revelation, we can say that this claim to have direct knowledge of totally revealed reality is not borne out by the history of the Christian Church or of Christian theology. Such history is in fact more suggestive of a situation in which there is a mixture of the given from without and of interpretation from the human side; or of a reality who would not be known were he not to present himself to us, but in our knowledge of whom we betray human aberrations and misunderstandings.

What has to be noticed, then, even at this early stage in our discussion, is that the term 'revelation' may serve a variety of purposes: it may be used to describe what God was doing when the Word was made flesh—he was making himself known; it may refer to *what* is known, a content, a subject-matter generally acknowledged by believers; it may, finally, apply to what the individual knows, something specially revealed to him. All these senses are perhaps operative most of the time but the consequence is not utmost clarity.

The given of christology as the here-and-now Christ

It is possible, however, if we have strong existentialist sympathies particularly, to give yet another account of the given of christology, namely, it is the self-presentation of Christ to me, or to the Church, in the here-and-now. Such a view would criticize the three previous views for laying too much emphasis upon the place which past events occupy in the given of christology—by seeking it either in old records, in a minimal historical core in past events, or in some past self-revelation of God. The given of christology takes place in the encounter which we have with Christ in the reality of the existential situation, the point where we hear the Word preached concerning the crucified and risen One, and we respond in faith and obedience, and where we pass from unauthentic to authentic existence. Christology is then the analysis and explication of that immediately given situation, the delineation of its basic constituents and the elaboration of its implications. This view may be expressed within a very wide range of variants, from the extreme existentialist forms which are thought by their critics to reduce christology to a type of self-examination, or of contorted introversion, to those which express the situation in terms of the Word of God and see the given of christology as a here-and-now address of God to the believer. In grouping these several views together, we are not insensitive to the radical differences that separate them. But they are single in their emphasis upon the contemporaneity of the given with which we have to deal in christology, and it is an emphasis which we shall be obliged to retain in our final summary. In the hands of some of its exponents, however, this view has been either irresponsible in its disparaging of the historical elements in the Christian faith or at best equivocal in its assessment of the place to be assigned to the historical or the documentary within the given of christology. That disparagement and that equivocation must be corrected in our own final summary.

The complexity of the given of christology

What then are we to say about the given of christology? To begin with, I should want to suggest that we ought not to feel compelled to choose any single one of the four views outlined above, to the exclusion of the others, but look rather to a conclusion which somehow integrates them all. Thus, while the given of christology is a self-presentation of Christ in the immediacy of contemporary existence, and while this self-presentation is effected with singleness of purpose, namely, for the salvation of a human soul; it nevertheless will be exposed on analysis to be extremely complex in structure. If we define christology as rational reflection upon the person, nature and claims of him with whom we have to do when we make the confession, 'I believe in the Lord Jesus Christ', then in the process of such analysis the simple given reveals itself to be an amazing complexity. Here are some of the constituents of this complexity. There are the documents of the holy scriptures, which are still the ultimate source from which we derive all knowledge of Jesus Christ, and which continue to sustain such knowledge and the reflection we impose upon them. To deny scriptures a place within the given or the historicity of the events recorded within them is to forget the rock whence we were hewn. Another constituent element within the given for many of us now must be the biblical criticism which is so constantly with us in all our Christian thinking. There are, too, passages which will for ever be coloured for me because of something which Calvin, or Luther, or Barth, or Bultmann, or Vischer, or Ebeling, has written about them; and the given of christology is for me informed by that kind of statement of theirs. The creeds of the Church, and the continuing living witness of the Church are now built into the very fabric of the given from which we start. In the Reformed church, we somewhat pride ourselves on cutting away the tangle of tradition, forgetting both that tradition may be a genuine medium of interpretative insight and that by now we have created our own rather rigid traditions which have a greater rigidity for all our pretending that they do not exist. We must include within the complexity of this given also our own response. Christology happens only within a believing community, and the given upon which it rests is something which happens only to believers. This response, in obedience and love, in faith and worship, is therefore a constituent element of the initially given; and its presence there is an index to the existence of other constituents which might well be omitted or neglected.

There is, then, a *prima facie* singleness, simplicity and immediacy in the given which is a construct of a variety of constituent elements. There is, too, a compulsiveness and authority attaching to the *totality* of the given which requires of us the appropriate response of faith, obedience and love. To stop to argue in the face of such authority and compulsiveness; to ask whether it is not in fact an illusion, a deception of the senses, noises in the head taken for the voices of the angels—to do any of these things is to deny the Christ who comes to us in such immediacy and directness. But the moment we depart from the immediacy of this faithful, obedient and loving response, in order to analyse the constituent elements within the whole, certain consequences must be carefully watched. For example, we must not commit the pretence of carrying over into our theological analysis all the attitudes and responses appropriate to the specifically religious situation: theology is necessarily dependent upon faith, but it is not simply an extrapolation of faith. It has to be allowed the freedom to stand back, to criticize, to wonder, to question.

A still graver danger to watch is that of investing any one of the constituent elements of the given which yields itself to us in separation from the others in the process of analysis—the danger of investing any one of these with the ultimacy, the authority, the compulsiveness of the totality. The Chalcedonian christology may be a constituent in the given situation in which Christ here and now makes his offer of salvation to me or imposes some demand upon me; but it would be wrong to extricate this christology from this situation, to hypostatize it and assign to it the compulsive authority, the ultimate validity of Christ himself. The I-Thou philosophy of Martin Buber may elucidate and sharpen my understanding of Christ's address to me, but this fact does not justify the elaboration of this philosophy into a self-existent, autonomous system with final authority. So we may proceed, *mutatis mutandis*, with Heidegger's existentialism, Whitehead's philosophy of organism, or Collingwood's historical categories. In a sense, the history of theological controversy is the story of the way in which opponents have vied with one another in a passionate earnestness to find in the constituent elements of *their* given the definition, validity and ultimacy which are the attributes proper only to Christ himself. By that way we reach the point where to question a man's theological convictions is taken by him and implied by us to question his faith. We are today very close to the point of identifying faith with theology, and there is no greater source of bitterness in controversy.

2

THE METHOD OF CHRISTOLOGY

SYNOPSIS

Preliminary accounts of what method is:

1. The attitude adopted by the practitioners of a discipline towards their subject-matter (searching, appreciating, worshipping,
etc.).

2. The special 'logic' which some disciplines are thought to have.

3. The accepted 'short-cuts' in the discipline, not obvious to the
layman.

4. The tacit assumptions which govern the development of the
argumentation, and the accepted criteria of evidence.

5. Range of conclusion established in the discipline.

Concerning the method of christology, it is often claimed that it
is *unique*, but the uniqueness lies not so much in the total difference
of christological method from all other methods, but in the special
way in which a variety of methods are combined. These several
methods are:

1. Textual, critical.

2. Historical.

3. Sociological and geographical.

4. Liturgical.

5. Ethical.

Concluding examination of how the several methods affect one
another.

The Method of Christology

WHAT I have been calling the shape of christology is determined by three constituent elements—the given, the method
followed in the study and exposition of this given, and finally,
the models which are the media of description, analysis and
examination of the given. Our immediate concern now is with
the *method* of christology. Perhaps the proper starting-point is to
indicate what exactly we intend by the term, and what we wish
to comprehend within it. Such definition is all the more important at a time when most disciplines are becoming explicit and
self-conscious about their methods.

Method as attitude to the subject-matter of a discipline

At a first glance, all that may be intended by the term 'method'
may be the way the given of the discipline is handled, the attitude adopted by its practitioners. For example, if the given lies
in the field of one of the natural sciences, then a certain en-
quiring, experimental, searching attitude is demanded, an un-
willingness to rest short of the final explanation, a desire to
question old, established positions. If the given lies in the field
of the literary arts, then a certain feeling for the substance of
the material is necessary, a degree of empathy, of penetration
into the mind and feelings of the author; or in the visual arts,
into the aesthetic objects, the painting or the sculpture. So
too in the religious field, the case might run, it is only the wor-
shipper who can handle the material of faith. The sceptic
by the nature of the case is cut off from the very realities
with which he wishes to deal. Indeed much has been made,
in recent theology, of this notion that in order to study
theology, we must have a properly faith-ful attitude, even a
prayer-ful attitude. In Martin Buber's words, 'God is not
to be expressed but addressed'. Certainly, then, the attitude
of the practitioner is one element in the way he handles his
material.

31

Method as logic

Secondly, the logic employed must be a further very important element in the method associated with any discipline. A certain mystique has been building up around the notion of logic. At one time philosophers thought, and indeed some still do, that there is a single logic to cover all forms of human thought, namely, the Aristotelian; and that all forms of human argumentation and inference are subject to the laws of valid inference enunciated in the so-called traditional formal logic. Even when other forms of inference were recognized, the *universality* of the forms of inference, and of the laws governing them was never departed from. The result was that exercises in literary criticism, experimental physics, poetry, mathematics, theology and ethics, to name but a varied few of many possible areas of human endeavour, were expected to conform to the same laws of thought, the same principles of valid inference, and were judged accordingly. R. G. Collingwood in his *The Idea of History*[1] gives an interesting example of such methodological empire-building.

> And just as in the seventeenth and eighteenth centuries there were materialists who argued from the success of physics in its own sphere that all reality was physical, so among ourselves the success of history has led some people to suggest that its methods are applicable to all the problems of knowledge, in other words, that all reality is historical.

Collingwood adds at once, 'This I believe to be an error'.

When the notion of logic, however, was extended to include not only laws of inference but kinds of statement, and the principles governing their permissibility, the way was open for a more radical criticism of some disciplines, and even for a demolition of some of their central concepts and subject-matter, in a way which was impossible under the older interpretation of logic as governing the laws of thought. It is an old story now of how A. J. Ayer and the logical positivists reduced metaphysics and theology, not to mention ethics and aesthetics, to the status of non-sense; an old story, even, how the idea of language-games opened up new possibilities of understanding

---

[1] Oxford 1946, p. 209.

these forms of alleged non-sense, and led the way to the conception of different logics for different disciplines. Theology has not been slow to seize the occasion of this respite to establish with considerable address and precision the claim to a specific way of thinking and arguing peculiar to its own subject-matter. How far this process may legitimately be carried in the exposition of theological method is a question which we propose shortly to examine; but for the moment the point stands that an essential constituent of any method is the logic followed in developing the discipline, the kinds of statement that are permissible, as well as the laws of inference that may be appealed to in validating an argument within the discipline.

Methodic short-cuts and 'peculiar logic'

It may be worth while to observe in this connection that the logic that governs arguments within a discipline is not always explicitly stated. In fact such arguments are full of what we might call logical short-cuts, series of steps within the longer process of inference which are simply omitted because they have become self-evident for the practitioners of a discipline. The process is readily observed in an orderly system such as Euclidean geometry, where conclusions reached by elaborate propositional proof in the earlier theorems are embodied as constituent parts of latter demonstrations, and have, by that time, become virtually self-evident. It requires an almost unnatural process of thought to prove that opposite angles of intersecting straight lines are equal. The process is not so easily observed in less orderly disciplines, but without it no discipline could make any progress whatsoever. Two comments may briefly be made on this process. The first is that revolutions tend to take place in any discipline when these long-unexamined processes of submerged argumentation are unearthed and shown to be false. The second comment is that the existence of this kind of short-cut argumentation is part-explanation of what is, to some extent at least, a delusion, namely, that every discipline has its own quite peculiar logic. In many cases, these short-cuts as I have been calling them, when set out in long-hand, can be seen to conform to ordinary sorts of logic, the simple traditional logic or one of the inductive logics. The basic process is in no way different from the variety of short-cuts which the experts have developed. Theology is as guilty of this type of short-cut as any other discipline; but it is emphatically not alone in this condition. Its presence in any discipline compels exponents to be extremely careful in the elaboration of the steps of their arguments for the benefit of the layman.

Tacit assumptions a part of method

There are, however, certain other rather vaguer considerations which might be immediately thought to be part of method, but which certainly are relevant to the way in which any practitioner handles the material of his discipline. Primary among these must be the tacit assumptions embodied in the premises from which he starts, assumptions of which he may not be even barely conscious, assumptions, on the other hand, which may be long-established starting-points which he has never seen fit to question. Those assumptions both limit the kinds of answer which he may give to his problems, and determine the questions that can be raised. In some cases they may even so prescribe the character of reality itself that entities which fall outside the limits defined have to be rejected as illusory or hallucinatory.

One of the most important of these assumptions is the conception of the evidence that is to be regarded as valid or relevant or permissible within the discipline—the evidence, that is, that is thought good enough to establish the conclusions to which the whole discipline is directed. The question of evidence is one of those most hotly debated by Christians with non-Christians. Are the Gospel narratives permissible as historical evidence, or are they presented with so much prejudice and acknowledged selection that they are to be disregarded in any accurate assessment of primitive Christianity? Or again, is the world of inner experience, the world of religious experience, so influenced by the subconscious, or even socio-economic pressures, that it cannot be allowed as a reliable guide to anything but the state of the human psyche at any given moment? But the question of evidence is by no means confined to debates of Christians with non-Christians. It appears as the central question in many legal cases. It is never very far away from the sphere of international politics, whether the issue be underground nuclear testing in Siberia or trade relations with Cuba or Cyprus. In most political arguments, the controversy is really centred around the question of evidence—whether a certain political judgment is borne out by the evidence or contradicted by it; whether the conclusions expressed do in fact follow from the evidence agreed to by both sides; and so on.

In philosophical discussions now for thirty years at least, the question of the nature of evidence has been fully examined under the name of verification. In what ways are different kinds of propositions to be verified? Is one way applicable to all, or does the character of the discipline determine exclusively the form of verification to be applied to its subject-matter? It would be wrong to suggest that the problem of evidence is coterminous with that of verification. Some ways of verification may not entail the production of what would normally be called evidence. For example, *reductio ad absurdum* forms of verification may require nothing that is positively evidence; the closest approximation to it is a state of affairs which negates the absurd consequence. Yet as we proceed to think out the problems raised for theology by the controversy over verification, it may be of value to remember that the question about verification may be most readily handled as a case of pertinent and permissible evidence rather than as a case of a peculiar type of inference.

Method related to range of conclusion

Another aspect of method which deserves mention is the range of conclusion which the discipline expects to reach; or if it may be stated in yet more general terms, the general conception of what the discipline is about, or what it is up to. This conception is by no means a fixed quantity. At one time, as has been so fully pointed out by E. L. Mascall[1] and I. T. Ramsey,[2] science was conceived of as presenting a pictorially accurate account of the true nature of reality, the models employed in scientific theories being more adequate photographs of entities which the human senses because of their insensitivity could not perceive. The exact relation of scientific theory to reality may still be a subject of intense debate, but however the participants

[1] *Christian Theology and Natural Science*, Longmans 1956, pp. 47ff.
[2] *Models and Mystery*, Oxford University Press 1964, *passim*.

may disagree in other directions, in this they are at one, in rejecting the photograph theory of scientific description. Particularly in physics is it the case that the ultimate conception of what the science is about is effectively transforming the method of the science itself. Psychology, in previous centuries, may have regarded itself as the science of mind, the science which exposes the nature of the self; yet, as research proceeds, the science has come to accept less ultimate, less ambitious aims, contenting itself with an analysis of the processes that take place within the mind, with the motives that condition behaviour and with the drives and instincts that maintain life itself, rather than with photographic descriptions of mind itself or the pure Ego or some such ultimate reality. Ian Ramsey[1] has in a characteristically forthright way uttered this warning to those psychologists who forget that they too are not through their models directly describing reality:

> Let not psychology repeat the errors of a Kelvin: let not psychology sponsor picturing models and then repeat the pseudo-puzzles and tall stories which characterized physics in an earlier day. By all means let psychology have its mathematical models; but more than ever let psychology realize that its topic is a person who will never—logically never—be transparent to any or all models, still less covered completely by picturing models.

One might be forgiven for wondering whether the same kind of change is not making itself evident in theology too. The history of theology abounds in words designed to describe with great precision, and, it may be added, with near-omniscience, the nature and attributes of God. But it is significant that in modern theology there is a certain reluctance to indulge in this kind of comprehensive account of the divine reality. Even Karl Barth, who might leap to mind as a notable exception to this general statement and be regarded, with considerable justification, as a person who has left little yet to be said about God, is nevertheless well safeguarded against possible criticism in this respect. He has fully reinstated the paradox of the hidden-ness and the revealedness of God, so that our human descriptions in the nature of the case fail to penetrate God's hidden-ness;

[1] *Op. cit.*, pp. 28f.

whereas the very notion of revelation itself always carries the possibility of human misinterpretation, for the risen Christ may still be taken to be a gardener, even by one who loved him. The final element, then, for the purposes of our present discussion, constituting and determining the method of any discipline is this general idea of what it is up to, its conception of the kind of statement it thinks to be feasible within the limitations it has set itself, and its assessment of the kind of conclusion to which it may legitimately move, following upon the premises it has accepted.

The alleged uniqueness of christological method

When, then, we come to consider the method of christology, we shall expect to find a certain complexity of content within its structure; but we shall not perhaps be altogether prepared for the very strong claims that will be made for the complete *uniqueness* of this method. The chief claim for such uniqueness is the fact that the subject of this discipline is completely unique. He is very God of very God, of one substance with God himself. Even though he shares our human nature, being of one substance with us as touching our humanity; nevertheless it is a human nature without sin, though bearing our sinfulness, and totally obedient to God's will though suffering the penalty of human disobedience. Consequently, the point at which he is most completely one with us is the point also of dissimilarity. Otherwise redemption would be frustrated. While it has often been argued that the method of christology is consequently unique, the case is one which must be carefully stated in face of the fact that in the course of christological study we find ourselves employing a whole range of varying methods, no one of which is by itself unique. It may turn out that the uniqueness of christological method lies in the unique way in which these several methods combine in christology. That possibility we shall later examine.

For the moment, I want to set forth some at least of the methods we find ourselves employing in christology and of the consequences which follow from such employment; and this evidence must compel us to be more cautious than is usually the case in our expression of the uniqueness of christological method. It shall be my contention that the so-called christo-logical method is in fact a complex of several distinct methods.

Literary-critical methods part of christology

First of all, given the truth of the statement that the people of Israel were the people of the Book, and that this description is rightfully extended to the Christian Church; given too the central place which biblical scriptures play in all theological systems and doctrinal formulations; it is an immediate conse-quence that a necessary first element in christological method is literary-critical method. Every theological student knows that there are hard-and-fast grammatical and syntactical rules gov-erning the construction of Hebrew and Greek sentences; that these rules are of the same kind as, if not also at times even identical with, the rules that hold in secular literature; and that the penalties for breaking these laws are as unpleasant and in-escapable as they are in secular literature. (A call to the ministry has never yet been accepted, though frequently offered, as an excuse for a certain unconcern about the minutiae of Hebrew and Greek grammar and syntax.)

When we move away from this obvious situation, however, in two directions, the basic point is often forgotten. On the one hand, at the level of the actual words used in the Bible, a great myth has been building up in our time that biblical words behave in ways peculiar to themselves. Thus, they are thought to gather to themselves whole constellations of meanings, which are immediately to be evoked on every occasion on which these significant words occur; they are not allowed to occur in hum-ility and simplicity, but only and ever with their full ceremonial dress. As soon as we recognize the socio-contextual character of human language, we become aware that the meaning of words for speaker and listener, for writer and reader, is largely de-pendent upon the setting in which they occur and the purpose they were designed to serve. Agreed that many settings recur, and even where they change, there must be sufficient unity of purpose in the use of the words to justify their recurrence; nevertheless, words are not carefully assembled packages with listed contents, which can pass from speaker to hearer without loss of value, or even with sure promise of identification. While, therefore, biblical words occur at times in settings different from those in which, say, scientific words occur, still they behave in these settings as do other words in theirs, and further they are to be found in ordinary settings even within the Bible itself. There lies the danger of the theological word-book approach to the biblical records, that it induces us to think of the Bible as atoms of essential biblical concepts in some loose conjunction, instead of as a vehicle of communication by a person or persons to others all within specific social and political as well as economic, geographical and cultural contexts.

Dogmatic checks on criticism

On the other hand, it has been felt at various times in the modern period of biblical criticism, that some kind of dogmatic check ought to be put upon such criticism. Few of us would still adhere to the view that all forms of textual or literary criticism are inappropriately applied to the biblical material; but something of that attitude has lingered on in the minds of many who are a little uncertain about where the line is to be drawn beyond which criticism may not pass. For some, this line has to be drawn before the virgin-birth stories are shown, on purely literary-critical grounds, to be untenable. For others, the abandonment of such stories would cause no difficulty, but they on the other hand would hold out strongly for the resurrection stories in spite of the difficulties created by the comparison of the different accounts, and reject any attempt to discredit them on critical grounds for fear of endangering the truth of the resurrection itself. Whether we are completely aware of the fact or honest enough to acknowledge it, most of us have never quite faced the problem of how far we are willing to allow criticism to go. Yet in one sense, we must be prepared to give it its head, believing that since our faith comes ultimately to us through the scriptures, it stands or falls with them. This is not to say that all forms of criticism are equally permissible; some may be patently anti-theistic or naturalistic, and so be totally inappropriate to the biblical material. It is to insist, however, that literary and textual criticism must be retained as an integral part of christological method. Christology must constantly be returning to the original account we have of its subject-matter. It must be constantly re-examining the terms in which the Bible first described Jesus. It must be re-assessing the stories which the primitive Church recorded about him. For that re-examination and re-assessment there can be no substitute, and to it there can be no end.

Historical method in christology

Closely connected with the literary-critical method, and to some extent containing it within itself, historical method must be regarded as the second major constituent element in christological method. Cullmann once wrote[1]:

All Christian theology in its innermost essence is biblical history.

If we were to take this remark seriously, we should begin to realize that theological method has a great deal more in common with historical method than with the method of the natural sciences. This latter assimilation is one—I think unfortunate—consequence of an over-emphasis upon the claim that theology is a science. It certainly is not a natural science and one wonders whether it is any more of a science than is history. At any rate, I wish for the present to explore the element of historical method engrossed in christological method.

At the start there is the obvious similarity between Christian theology and historical study that they are both ultimately concerned with records, with their authenticity, and with the veracity and reliability of their authors. It cannot be stressed too strongly that the records hold this key position in theology in view of tendencies in two directions to reduce their importance. On the one hand, as a consequence of the introduction into contemporary theology of historical scepticism—which was so obvious a feature of the *Concluding Unscientific Postscript* of Kierkegaard and which has appeared in Barth's writings as well as Bultmann's for they have this common ancestor—there has resulted a quite drastic reduction of the minimum of acknowledged historical fact required to substantiate the Christian faith. The reality of this tendency towards historical scepticism has resulted in post-Bultmannian attempts to dehistoricize as well as to demythologize the faith.

[1] *Christ and Time* (ET), SCM Press 1951, p. 23.

The second tendency towards a reduction of the significance of the records comes from a quite different quarter, in fact from a point of extreme evangelicalism. It is the tendency so to emphasize the reality of the present experience of Jesus Christ that the authenticity of the records becomes an irrelevant question. In a recent discussion[1] with David Frost, Dr Billy Graham came very close to admitting that if modern criticism should disprove the truth of the Bible, his faith, now so deeply personal a relationship with a really present Christ, would be unaltered. One cannot but admire the depth of such personal conviction, but one may be forgiven for wondering how long this kind of personal relationship with Christ could be sustained without the reinforcing structure of the biblical literature and its narratives about Christ. My own guess is that without that structure this sort of personal experience would very soon become a rather formless, if not also joyless, mysticism. Of course, in the statement to which I have referred I do not believe that Dr Graham was really presenting his own true position. The man who is so often heard to say, 'The Bible says . . .' can be in no doubt about the part which the scriptures play in the creation and sustaining of his faith. To hold an historical faith is to have a faith which stands or falls with the records.

It is for that very reason that christological method like historical method has to be concerned with the detail of historical authenticity, and with the assessment of evidence; in fact, the reliability of the records is part of the case for the Christian faith. It is not sufficient to say that the scriptures are completely trustworthy in all matters of faith, life and doctrine, because what has been left unsaid carries strong negative implications. This view leaves open the possibility that in historical detail the scriptures may prove to be unreliable, and that consequence is disturbing. The teaching about faith, life and doctrine comes in the scriptures, in a hard shell of historical record; and if the shell is damaged, the contents at once become suspect. This is not to say that all the biblical narratives are factually accurate, nor is it to say that the order of events as recorded in the scriptures is precise in every case. But it is to say that we must be prepared to submit the narratives and the recorded series of

[1] On BBC television.

41

events to the most open-minded scrutiny of which we are capable. We must, too, be always ready for the possibility that it is not the recital of chronological data that is necessarily closest to fact; a slightly disordered gossipy narrative may take us closer to the heart of what happened, and it is with 'what happened' that we are concerned in historical method rather than with a bald, unvarnished statement of fact.

Mediation in christology

It is for this very reason that R. G. Collingwood in his *The Idea of History* insists that it is knowledge of the past rather than chronological recording which is the true task of the historian. This knowledge is an imaginative process in which the historian re-enacts the thought of agents in the historical past. It is a process in which he reconstructs the motivational patterns that underlay the overt behaviour of figures of the past. It is a process of rational integration of isolated items of evidence, so that they find their place within an explanatory system without being rationalized away. The historian's task is, so to speak, to know *now* what happened *then* through records that exist in the present but have their meaning, their substance, their reality in the past. To use his language, the records are the media of historical immediacy. They create the context in and through which the past is re-lived in the present. Admittedly Collingwood's account of history and of historical knowledge carries overtones of idealistic philosophy; it evinces, too, a degree of subjectivism which he may never manage to avoid. But it has so many close connections with christological method that we may be well rewarded for finding in it an ally in the exposition of christological method. For christology, the records mediate a figure of the past, so that he becomes a reality in the present. This mediation is an endemic feature of the christological situation; to try to escape from it results only in the creation of a mental or spiritual substitute for the real Christ. The development of christological reflection is a progressive determination of the factual detail of the person and work of Jesus Christ, of the penetration into depth of the narrative accounts of the sciptures. At the centre of every christological statement is an historical statement endeavouring to make its escape. When the

42

historical statement fails to appear, we may well ask ourselves whether we really have been dealing with a christological statement.

The unique historical person, Jesus Christ

It would be wrong to conclude this brief comparison of christological method with historical method, without mentioning the point of similarity of which most is made in popular accounts of the matter, namely, that as historical research has to do with the unique and the unrepeatable in human affairs, christological study deals with him who is absolutely unique, the God-man, who differentiates himself so completely from all else in human history. J. V. Langmead Casserley[1] described the unique event, or person, with which theology along with history, metaphysics, poetry and drama have to deal, as the singular; and thereby drew attention to the logical oddness of this category, which was neither logical universal nor logical particular, which was not a member of a class-universal, but something logically different from both. The point was well-made, and it was a comfort to theologians to know that their logical troubles were shared by historians, metaphysicians and others. But all the problems were not solved because a uniqueness attaches to the event of the incarnation which is different from that attaching to 'first to climb Everest', and we obscure *this* uniqueness if we assimilate it to those other forms of the singular. Nevertheless, there is a uniqueness in the field of the historical which is foreign to the natural sciences; and it is on this ground that we would take historical method as the more reliable clue to theological method than any other.

Geographical elements in christological method

Once the part which historical method plays within christology is established, certain immediate consequences follow. The subject of christology, the God-man, Jesus Christ, lived in a certain part of the world and in a certain society. It is inevitable therefore, that geographical and sociological considerations will affect the judgments which we pass upon the historical events in the Gospel narrative. It is rather significant that when theo-

[1] *The Christian in Philosophy*, Faber and Faber 1948.

logy was more outspokenly insistent than it is now upon the humanity of Christ, intense interest was taken in the geography of the Holy Land. The *mise-en-scène* of the incarnation was of great importance, for this was a human life, lived upon earth and in the midst of a nation in the eastern Mediterranean area. Geographical details were of relevance both to the form which the life took and to the character it bore. But once a degree of scepticism concerning the historical detail of the incarnation began to be expressed, as we have seen under the influence of Kierkegaardian existentialism; once the deity of Christ was reaffirmed in classical Chalcedonian terms; there came, it might appear almost automatically, a lessening of interest in the geographical circumstances of the incarnation.

Sociological analysis has also a contribution to make in laying bare the main features both of the society in which Christ lived, and in assessing the characteristics of the Christian community which grew out of the fact of the incarnation and within which the records were produced to present the story of this fact in all the freshness of its original impact. Once again we are in danger of so emphasizing the divine character of the Church that we neglect its human sociological features. There is a docetism in the doctrine of the Church no less than in christology. So long as it is affirmed that the Church is the body of Christ in the world, so long will there be a place for sociological method in the understanding of how that Church has developed and of how it has formed the records which are the basis of all christological formulation. In short, then, the fact of the incarnation compels us to acknowledge that part at least of christological method must be devoted to the examination of the geographical and the sociological aspects of the situation in which it took place; and that the method of such study must bear close affinity to the kind of investigation that we give to such subjects in more secular connections. To say otherwise is to endanger what Barth calls the 'earthly' character of the incarnation.

Liturgical method and christology

If we pursue a little further the idea that sociological considerations are pertinent to christological method, we very soon discover that one of the chief functions, indeed the highest function, of this community created by the incarnation, is to worship God. When the christological subject-matter is approached, it has to be borne in mind that we are dealing with a person towards whom the proper attitude is not one of scientific curiosity, or detached inquisitiveness, but ultimately one of worship and adoration, trust and obedience. Clearly when handling the christological material, it will be unnatural, strained and somewhat unrealistic for us to try to maintain a reverent attitude of adoration and faithful obedience. We may have to suspend for a time the commission under which we stand as the bondsmen of Christ to go at once into all the world and preach the Gospel, or tend the hungry, the suffering and the underprivileged brethren for whom he died. We may simply have to do so in order to understand more fully what his nature is who commissions us. But we have to recognize that the kind of thinking that we do when such suspension takes place is second-order thinking, and that the primary relationship to Christ is that of obedience, trust, adoration and supremely love.

This liturgical element—I use the term in its all-inclusive sense of 'relating to worship', and not solely in reference to *orders* of worship—conditions the form of christological method at a number of specifiable points. For example, to begin with, we shall not be satisfied with any christological analysis which eliminates from its conception of who he is all valid basis for an attitude of worship to him. It is on this very score that humanistic interpretations of the person of Jesus Christ fail, that they present to us someone who cannot sustain human *worship*; admiration, perhaps, even a sense of wonder at the courage he had in the face of danger and death, but never worship. That is given only to God. The questions with which the liturgical interest will always tax any christological analysis will, therefore, be: How easily does the analysis integrate with a living situation in which the believer trusts, loves and obeys Jesus Christ? To what degree is the analysis organically united with the worship of Christ, so that it may finally come to inform, to deepen and enrich the worship of Christ? This is the final test of any christology, whether it can become part of that offering of himself to the Father which Christ makes at the centre of all truly Christian worship.

We shall expect next that something of this liturgical interest will manifest itself in the records which we have noted as forming a central part of the christological subject-matter. It will appear in the very purpose of the documents themselves, for they were designed not to be read as literature, nor even as history, but in order that men and women through them should come to be saved in knowing and being known of the Christ of whom they tell us. As has already been observed, it is not implied that because of this overriding purpose, the documents bear no literary characteristics, or that they will be any the less historical. Indeed without the literary form and without at least a measure of historical accuracy, they would not serve the liturgical purpose.

The liturgical interest expresses itself in yet other ways. Some excerpts may be taken directly from the records and embodied in a modern act of worship: Eph. 1.3ff., for example—'Blessed be the God and Father of our Lord Jesus Christ, who hath blessed us with all spiritual blessings in heavenly places in Christ', or Rom. 16.25-27, or II Cor. 1.3ff., may all be the very words we use in order to worship God here and now. We have, too, the whole continuing practice whereby a text is made the basis of a sermon, so that a word spoken to someone two thousand years ago or even more may be at this very moment the means by which Christ speaks again to his people. This re-emergence of Christ contemporaneously with the preached word demonstrates to us that the documents of scripture are not themselves the totality of our subject-matter, and also that christological method is not one simple approach to a completely uniform body of material. At the same time, the liturgical interest may be so dominant in the mind of the authors of the original documents, that the clue to their structure is to be found in the liturgical purpose they serve. Archbishop Carrington, for example, has adopted the thesis that the shape of the Christian year has been imposed upon the Gospel according to St Mark, and that its literary form is meaningless without this clue. The Gospel according to St John obviously bears the marks of much editing, but it is important to remember that this editing is not simply for the purpose of producing a document with a distinctive literary polish, particularly when compared with, for example, the Gospel according to St Mark, but rather in order to enable readers to enter into the right relation to him, who is the way, the truth and the life.

Ethics and christology

My general contention, then, has been that christological method is a complex of different methods, the historical, the literary-critical, the sociological and the liturgical. There is one other component in this method which I should still like to add to those already named: the ethical method. Perhaps it is not inappropriate after some fifty years and more to quote P. T. Forsyth[1]:

> The modern moralization of religion thus prescribes a new manner of enquiry on such a central subject as the person of Jesus Christ. . . . Now concerning the union of the two natures in Jesus Christ the old dogma thought in a far too natural and non-moral way. Its categories were too elemental and physical. It conceived it as an act of might, of immediate divine power, an act which united the two natures *into* a person rather than *through* that person. . . . There can be no unity of spirits like God and man except in a moral way, by personal action which is moral in its method as well as in its aim.

The moralization of religion which P. T. Forsyth seems to take so much for granted in this passage has not proceeded with the steady progress which he anticipated. For example, the what I might call subordination of ethics to dogmatics has impeded somewhat the penetration of the ethical categories into the whole range of dogmatic thought; in fact, in this subordination, ethics becomes the derivative discipline, introduced almost too late in the process to exert any controlling influence. More seriously for christology, the reduction of the size of the historical picture of Jesus Christ, which has been a feature not solely of Bultmannian christology but largely of all christologies influenced by Kierkegaardian historical scepticism, has led to a proportional diminution of the conception of the strictly ethical aspects of the person of Christ. This process, in conservative circles at least, has contained an element of reaction against the almost exclusively ethical and non-dogmatic account of Christ

[1] *The Person and Place of Jesus Christ*, Hodder and Stoughton 1911, pp. 222f.

47

which was given by liberal theology. Christ the great moral teacher or Christ the embodiment of perfect morality has been replaced by Christ, the Word made flesh or Christ the supreme revelation of the very being of God himself. It is important, then, to recognize the danger which Forsyth saw in previous christologies—that the introduction of the classical christological categories might lead to the possibility of non-moral ways of understanding Christ's nature, and to insist that ethical method must find a place as part of christological method.

We are inclined, perhaps, to attach too much importance to the moralizing of theological categories, as if it were a modern phenomenon. R. V. Sellers[1] writes:

> (The Antiochenes) are supremely interested in man the moral being, and in particular concentrate on his power of self-determination. But it is important to notice that the conception of man as a free spirit is never considered in isolation, but always against the background of the thought of God's purpose for him. They may be called anthropologists, but their anthropology is intimately associated with their ethical and soteriological ideas. Whatever then, be the errors which the Antiochenes otherwise commit, e.g. that they affirm a Duad of Sons, at least in their conception of the humanity of Christ they stood firmly in the tradition of the scriptures themselves in contending for the genuineness of the humanity of Christ.

So, too, before we reject Theodore of Mopsuestia's idea that the union of God and man in Jesus Christ is only rightly understood as a moral union, such as that of man and wife, we must remember not only that he is here speaking analogically, but also that in a matter such as this probably an ethical category is more appropriate than a purely metaphysical one.

Christological method composed of a variety of contributory methods

I wish now to draw together the main conclusions that seem to be emerging from this general discussion of the constituent elements in christological method, or of what I have at times spoken of as the several methods which taken together constitute the christological method.

Perhaps the first immediately noteworthy point is that it is

[1] *The Council of Chalcedon*, SPCK 1953, p. 164.

very difficult, if not impossible, to maintain that there is a peculiar and proper christological method different and distinct from those constituent methods which I have named. The positive form of this assertion is that christological method is a peculiar and specific complex of these constituent methods, and as such is not reproduced in any other disciplines—in spite of the fact that most of these methods appear in other disciplines. The enumeration of these constituent methods enables us to see how easily any one of them may usurp authority and at once present a radically distorted or gravely diminished account of the christological subject-matter. At one time or another in the history of doctrine or culture, this is exactly what has happened —when sociologists have presented the fact of Christ in terms of Judaic social, economic and political pressures; when literary-critics or form-critics reduced the documents of Christian scriptures to a fragment of their proper size; when scientific historians sought in these documents for the evidence of uncommitted and detached by-standers; when liberals drew a picture of the perfect man or offered an account of the fully-adjusted personality; or even when the liturgist constructed christology solely in relation to the worship of the Christian Church, hoping to save it from the humiliation of bitter controversy. This complexity of method accounts not only for the differences in approach between Christians and non-Christians, but also for the quite radical differences that occur between Christians. Some have one overriding interest, and others another, with the result that we have a variation as wide as that between Dibelius in his *Jesus* and Brunner in his *The Mediator*, or between B. Barton's *The Man Nobody Knew* and Bornkamm's *Jesus of Nazareth*.

The complexity of method which is said to characterize christology may be illustrated also from the complexity of the different items which to begin with we discovered in any method. The first of these which we mentioned[1] was that of attitude. At once we notice that while Christ is the subject of Christian worship and devotion and consequently requires of us constant obedience and trust, nevertheless there must be a place within christology for a more questioning attitude. It must be possible to stand back, as it were, and critically review the

[1] Above, p. 31.

documents, the literary forms, the narratives, the hymns, the confessions of faith, in order to determine their authenticity and their veracity. It will be necessary also to compare the ethical aspects of Jesus' teaching with that of moral teachers of other times, in order to bring out its essentially distinctive character; but that process of comparison will entail a considerable suspension of the urgency of his moral imperatives. In other words it will involve something of the attitude of the moral philosopher. And so we begin to observe that elements of the attitudes proper to the different methods constitutive of christological method are embodied in the attitude adopted in christology. The same is true of the logic employed in christology. It should by now be clear that there is not one peculiar christological logic, but that according to the kind of problem we are trying to solve, or the sort of aspect of the christological situation we are seeking to describe, or even defend, the logic we employ will in fact vary somewhat.

When we go on to such things as the tacit assumptions accepted in any method, the evidence and types of verification that are permissible, or even to the conclusions anticipated from the use of the method, it appears at a first glance that we have moved into areas where special 'religious' considerations might be expected to overrule all others. For example, when the application of the standards of evidence acceptable in historical study seemed to be destroying the historical foundation of the Christian Gospel by disproving the historicity of the events of Christ's life, it might seem necessary to invoke some non-historical sanctions to restrain the historical method. Or if psychological analysts seemed to be proving that Jesus was a schizophrenic or a paranoic, then the theological claims concerning his deity might seem to have to be invoked to secure the integrity of his personality. Or even when the moral philosopher was approaching a decision in favour of the ethics of Plato as against that of Jesus, a rejection of justification by works or an exposition of the greater importance of the death of Jesus than that of Socrates might be suddenly summoned up to redress the balance on the Christian side.

Two replies must, I feel, be made to extreme measures. On the one hand, we have to face the fact that any one of these possible, as we believe, misinterpretations of the person of Jesus Christ may be correct. It is a logical possibility that Jesus may have been a schizophrenic, that he may have taught an ethic which was less adequate than Plato's, or indeed that he may not have existed at all. The existence of this logical possibility is part of the fact that he entered human history and exposed himself to the ambiguities both of history and of historical interpretation. It is against the background of this logical possibility that faith is to be characterized as faith and never as sight. The atheist construes the logical possibility as reality, while the fanatic is in danger, at the other end of the scale, of converting faith into sight and claiming incontrovertible certainty on all points.

On the other hand it would be wrong to leave the impression that the ultimate decision between the possibility of the truth of these propositions being contradictory of Christianity and the authenticity of Christian faith lies with a peradventure of faith, even when this peradventure is reinforced with a high doctrine of the Holy Spirit. Such is a burden more heavy than human faith and decision can rightly be called upon to endure. There is an alternative: namely, that within and among the several methods which, we have argued, are constitutive of christological method there operates a system of checks and balances so that the final construction is one which is in agreement with the substance of the faith. The existence of such a system is not in itself a reason why the atheist ought to use it, for he would no more wish to do so than a tone-deaf person might choose to argue about the cadences in a piece of music. Nor does the existence of the system eliminate all occasion of disagreement among Christian theologians, for they will still argue about the adjustment of the checks and balances. The important point is, however, that they will argue within the system and expect to convince their fellows by drawing upon evidence from within it and employing inferences that are valid within it. What they ought not try to do is to escape from the system into a christological method which claims to stand above and apart from all the others we mentioned and to have veridical knowledge on all the questions at issue. Some theologians may try to do so, but they will go out by the front door only to re-enter by the back door; for they too must in the end speak of documents and history, of ethics and psychology, of liturgy and logic. At that point they have returned to the fold, and we are perhaps just a little relieved that they have found it necessary to do so. They might have been right!

3

MODELS IN CHRISTOLOGY

SYNOPSIS

Variety of names and titles given to Jesus Christ in scriptures and creeds.

Professor Ian Ramsey on Models (*Models and Mystery*):

1. Distinction between 'picturing models' which endeavour to be replicas of reality and 'disclosure models' which provide techniques for talking about reality, and are the media through which reality discloses itself.

2. Comparison of use of models in science and use of models in theology: similarities and differences. In both cases the model provides insight into reality.

Variety of functions served by models in christology:

1. Disclosure is basis of a claim which Christ makes upon us in a specific direction, and is never therefore expendable, never 'merely' a metaphor.

2. Ontological reference of model.

3. Descriptive function of model raises question of the relation of model to analogy.

4. Normative importance of models is to be emphasized in view of equivocal status of confessions and subordinate standards in Protestant churches.

5. Integrative function of models is seen in the way in which they pervade theological construction, providing a repetitive pattern for conflating a variety of doctrines. The model of unity.

Models in Christology

ONE FEATURE of Christian worship which even the most callous familiarity cannot fail to observe is the sheer variety of titles ascribed to Jesus Christ. They range from the list which is part of the Old Testament Advent lesson, Isa. 9.6: 'And his name shall be called Wonderful, Counsellor, The mighty God, The everlasting Father, The Prince of Peace' to the great climax of phrases contained in the Nicaeo-Constantinopolitan Creed: 'And in one Lord Jesus Christ, the only-begotten Son of God, Begotten of his Father before all worlds, God of God, Light of Light, Very God of Very God, Begotten not made, Being of one substance with the Father, By whom all things were made: Who for us men and for our salvation came down from heaven, And was incarnate by the Holy Ghost of the Virgin Mary. And was made man.' Within the limits of this wide range there lie the names which occur within the Gospels themselves, where Jesus is described, or rather describes himself, as the way, the truth, the life, the shepherd, the vine, ransom, and so on; as well as the many titles which later theology has employed—leader, hero and religious genius.

Clearly, the use of such a variety of titles creates problems for biblical students, who must decide, for example, which of the New Testament terms are going to have precedence over others; how far contemporary Jewish usage or previous Old Testament usage or even classical usage is to be allowed to predetermine the interpretation of New Testament terms; and whether there are irreconcilable differences of emphasis when the terminology favoured by one evangelist is compared with that of another. In approaching the question of the place of models in christology, obviously we shall be obliged to keep these biblical problems in mind; but the issues that confront us here are slightly different. It is clear, for example, that we cannot rest content with a view which simply adds these different titles together, as if they were all obviously compatible descriptions of an immediately observable entity or person. They are

55

drawn from vastly different contexts; they carry a seemingly endless variety of implications and refer to a wide range of situations. It is therefore necessary to evolve some account of how they are uniformly affirmed of the same subject without contradiction and without ultimate confusion. Some consideration will have to be given of the purposes which are served by the variety of titles applied to Jesus Christ. They are not simply proper names for him nor are they only denotative; they are in some sense descriptive of who he is and of the part he plays in the will of God for the salvation of mankind. In short, we shall have to ask *what* these titles are. The quick answer to that question is that titles of the sort we have been mentioning are the models with which the christological method operates in dealing with its given, its subject-matter. Our present task then is to indicate what the term 'model' means in this application; to specify the various sources and functions of models, and particularly of christological models; and to indicate the part which they play in defining the character of theological language.

Ian T. Ramsey's views on models

Ian T. Ramsey has recently[1] drawn together a number of views on models, and contributed on his own side a very illuminating analysis of their nature and function particularly in relation to theology. We may best begin by reviewing what he has to say.

Basic to his whole position is a distinction between 'picturing models' and 'disclosure models' or, as Professor Max Black would call them, 'analogue models'. The former featured prominently in the scientific theory of Lord Kelvin's day. The models which science employed were thought to be replicas or copy-pictures of whatever it was they were modelling. Models serve a rather different purpose in modern science: they form 'a collection of distinctive, reliable, and easily specifiable techniques for talking about a reality which is ultimately mysterious'.[2] There are, as it were, three elements in the situation: first, the phenomena which have constituted a problem for the scientist and defy either explanation or description in terms of known laws, principles or hypotheses; secondly, the model which dis-

---

[1] In *Models and Mystery* (Whidden Lectures), 1964.   [2] *Op. cit.*, p. 4.

plays some structural similarity to the phenomena; and thirdly, a theory or deductive system of a very complex nature associated with the phenomena, from which certain fundamental notions are selected in the model for simplified treatment. Professor Ramsey speaks of the relation of the model to the phenomena in a variety of ways in addition to that of isomorphism already mentioned. For example, the models 'chime in with and echo'[1] the phenomena; and as a consequence of this relation, they are together associated in a disclosure, a disclosure about some mystery in the universe. While the idea that models are descriptive[2] is rejected, it is equally strongly affirmed that the disclosure of which is the model is a medium entails both a deeper understanding of the reality disclosed and a degree of ontological commitment to it. In other words, the model is not a figment of the imagination nor is it a precise picture, but it does enable us to be articulate about some aspect of the universe.

There is a sufficiently far-reaching parallel, Professor Ramsey thinks, between models in science and models in theology to justify description of the latter in terms of the former. To begin with, the phenomena which constituted the events of the life, death and resurrection of Jesus Christ were so complex and involved, and the minds of Christ's followers were still so far removed from precise theological definition, that models were called in to give immediate interpretation to the phenomena. They provide a basis for conversation concerning the phenomena and for the further proclamation of them without anticipating the precision of later dogmatic formulae. Again, where the phenomena are particularly complex, the models may single out specific aspects of them and so enable an understanding of them which would otherwise prove impossible. So, too, religious models, drawn from the universe or man's experience of it, must so chime in with the religious phenomena which they model as to create a disclosure situation, yielding insight and understanding. While it is not possible to verify a religious model by means of any deductive inferences which we may draw from them, a practical test is not altogether wanting, in that it may be shown to incorporate a wide range of relevant phenomena and meet a variety of practical needs. This test is

----

[1] *Op. cit.*, p. 13. [2] *Op. cit.*, p. 20.

called 'empirical fit' by Professor Ramsey. It is an aspect of models which we shall endeavour to demonstrate is of immense contemporary importance.

Later on[1] Professor Ramsey draws on a more literary interpretation of models when he compares them with metaphors, but secures roughly the same result as that yielded by his investigation of scientific models. Metaphor involves the juxtaposition and consequent interpenetration of two contexts in such a way as to produce fresh disclosure which includes both within itself. Alternatively, metaphor is 'a tangential meeting of two diverse contexts'[2] in such a way that discourse concerning one is facilitated and enriched through the application to it of the terms of discourse of the other. Once again, the metaphor yields deeper insight into a mystery which would otherwise elude our grasp; the metaphor is the medium of disclosure of a reality which, or who, claims our commitment. There is then no doubt about the objective reference of the metaphor, but it is not the objective reference of precise description. There is a 'logical gap between the model and what the insight reveals, between the model and the situation in which it is fulfilled'.[3] It is the existence of this gap which prevents the metaphor from being descriptive or pictorial. It is the combination of the metaphor and the original in a single insight which secures for the metaphor a role in the understanding of objective reality. Once again the relation between metaphor and religious language is shown by Professor Ramsey to be of prime importance. It is possible to see much of the language of theology as metaphorical, and to hold that the various metaphors which theology employs continue to yield 'cosmic disclosures', in short to be the literary media of divine revelation. They point to the mystery which even in disclosure retains its mysteriousness.

I have stated Professor Ramsey's views at such considerable length for two reasons. The first and obvious one is that it is a remarkably penetrating and imaginative account of the nature and function of models in theological discourse. The second is that this book, of an importance far beyond its size, has served to direct my own thoughts on the subject in ways which Pro-

[1] In chapter 3, *op. cit.*   [2] *Op. cit.*, p. 52.
[3] *Op. cit.*, p. 59.

fessor Ramsey did not intend and which are not necessarily extensions of his thought but which would make little sense without his account before us.

There would appear to be several basic problems relating to models—their nature, their logical status and their function particularly in theology and christology; and I propose to begin by examining the variety of functions which they perform. It is hoped that we shall thereby drive a road through to some clearer conception of their nature and status in the christological context.

Models as media of disclosure

With Professor Ramsey's account in front of us it is impossible not to start off with the function of *disclosure*. Perhaps it is absolutely right to lay the emphasis primarily on this function of the models, namely, that they exist to serve God himself, to be the media by which he is to be known, worshipped and obeyed. Far too often the question of models is seen as a logical question, of how human language can penetrate to the heart of the divine mystery, of how a linguistic extrapolation is achieved so that, with human grammar and syntax, we are able to speak of God himself. But they are, on the contrary, moments in the divine self-disclosure, part of the way in which he addresses himself to us, and declares his purpose for our lives. This fact must override all that we say about models; and we must constantly remind ourselves of it particularly when we are in danger of being immersed in the logical details to which we are now required to direct ourselves.

Take, for example, the way in which the disclosure might be said to take place. When Professor Ramsey is talking of scientific models, he says that there is a certain isomorphism between the phenomena in the ordinary world and the models, which when the one is applied to the other yields a disclosure of some reality beyond them both. It is necessary to cash the values of this abstract account of the matter to see clearly what it implies.

Let us consider, for example, the situation in which Christ's authority inspired the centurion[1] to believe that Christ would cure his sick servant. The actual phenomena in this case would

[1] Luke 7.1ff.

59

be the outward bearing of Christ, some word the centurion had heard, or the inward peace which shone from the face of Christ. The model would be the centurion's own exercise of authority. 'For I also am a man set under authority, having under me soldiers; and I say to one, Go, and he goeth; and to another, Come, and he cometh; and to my servant, Do this, and he doeth it.'[1] A certain isomorphic relationship between Christ's behaviour and his position yielded the disclosure, which took an interesting form. For the centurion did not say, as if concluding an argument, 'And so I observe that you hold a position of very high authority and are able to command whatsoever you wish, confident that it will be executed.' Instead, he stated the practical consequence which Christ's possession of that authority entailed for the present situation. 'Say in a word, and my servant shall be healed.'[2] The Gospels abound in examples. In John 10.1ff., Jesus speaks of a good shepherd who goes before his sheep, and whom they follow; the good shepherd whose voice they know; the one who will finally give his life for his sheep. To check progress to this point, we may say that there are three elements in the model-situation; the phenomena in the everyday world, the model and the subject of disclosure, to which we are directed through the association of model and phenomena. The most significant example of all is perhaps the occasion of the institution of the sacrament of the Lord's Supper. At Luke 22.19, 20 we read:

> And Jesus took bread, and gave thanks, and brake it, and gave unto them saying, This is my body which is given for you: this do in remembrance of me.
> Likewise also the cup after supper, saying, This cup is the new testament in my blood, which is shed for you.

These verses, when looked at in terms of the logic of models, are of great interest, chiefly for two reasons. First we do not have one but a series of models in both cases. We begin on each occasion with phenomena, in v. 19, the giving of bread, and in v. 20, the offering of the cup of wine. Model one, in v. 19, is the breaking of the body of Christ; and model two is the vicarious sacrifice involved in the breaking of the body of Christ, and the

---

[1] V. 8.   [2] V. 7b.

ultimate disclosure, the soteriological purpose served by these events. In v. 20, a third model is inserted with the words, 'the new testament', the initiation by God of a new relation to fulfil the promise contained in the old covenant that God had made with Israel. But the final disclosure is the same, God's purpose of salvation for those who receive the sacrament. If we follow the account of the institution of the sacrament of the Lord's supper as recorded by St Paul in I Cor. 11.23ff., we find the recurrence of an aspect of the model situation which we noticed in the account of the healing of the centurion's servant (Luke 7.1ff.), namely, the practical act. The end-term of the series of models and of the final disclosure enshrined in the celebration of the sacrament is not simply disclosure of a truth, even the highest soteriological truth, but the eating and the drinking, the receiving of the Body and Blood of Jesus Christ. The second point of interest about the models used in the institution of the sacrament is that they converge on the same disclosure, or more precisely, on the disclosure of the same reality, the single purpose of God. It might be called a 'hinge disclosure' because both series of models depend upon it for their validity and indeed for their meaning, and because however free and open the series may be at the phenomena end, it has to be firm and fixed at the disclosure end.

When Professor Ramsey moves to the comparison of models and metaphors, he retains the triadic structure which we have mentioned above. A metaphor occurs when two contexts are allowed to interpenetrate so that terms applicable within the range of the one are given a reference within the other. As before, this juxtaposition of contexts, this interpenetration generates a disclosure. It does so by *pointing* the understanding in the direction in which the disclosure is to be gained. When we examine the record of the institution of the sacrament of the Lord's Supper in the light of models as metaphors, we observe once again the importance of the fact that the models as metaphors point in the same direction and to the same subject. What is true in the immediately obvious way of the sacramental models must be equally true of the others. Linguistic and literary as well as logical chaos would result if the models pointed in many different directions, to many different subjects. It is for this reason of great importance to hold that the parables of the Kingdom (Matt. 13.24ff.) in spite of the diversity of the models —a man sowing good seed in his field (vv. 24ff.), a grain of mustard seed (vv. 31ff.), and leaven in meal (vv. 33ff.) point to a single reality. It is this uniform reference which saves them from being a kaleidoscopic series of prettily poetic pictures.

Theological and scientific models compared

It might be argued that theological models resemble metaphors more closely than they do the scientific models. When Jesus says, 'I am the door of the sheep',[1] he would appear to be using a metaphor, rather than a scientific model. Or again, 'I am the true vine, and my Father is the husbandman',[2] savours more of literary device than scientific inference. The case is, however, far from complete against the employment of the scientific approach to models. Professor Ramsey is careful to point out[3] that there are great differences between scientific models and theological models. For example, the scientific model is made the basis of precise deductions which subsequently become the subject of extensive experimentation for purposes of verification or falsification. The deductions result in conclusions relating to definite modes and quantities, and there can be no comparable element in the conclusions which theological models yield. Nor, we may now add, would it be right to regard theological models simply as hypotheses which stand or fall with the conclusions we deduce from them. They have an independence of existence and status which forbids such arbitrariness in our attitude to them. In other words, we cannot apply the concept of scientific model to the analysis of theological language without taking pains to illustrate the ways in which the two kinds of models differ from one another.

The question might well be asked whether models in theology are in any aspects different from literary metaphors. A provisional answer may be given at this stage. It is that while ontological reference is present in both there is a greater degree of ontological commitment to the former than to the latter. In a sentence embodying a metaphor, the commitment is to the subject compared with the metaphorical entity or concept. In

[1] John 10.7.   [2] John 15.1.   [3] *Op. cit.*, p. 16.

a sentence embodying a theological model, the model is itself part of the subject of commitment, and in some cases even prescribes the form of the commitment. For example, the model of shepherd as applied to Christ entails the commitment of trust, whereas if we talk of him who will be the judge of the quick and the dead, the commitment is one of humble submission to his judgment. From the fact, then, that theological models are not simply equivalent to scientific or literary models, we might be tempted half-humorously to say that we are employing models as models in the theological reference. Whether we have not in fact come rather close to interpreting theological models as analogies is a point to which we shall return. For my own part, I should be inclined to say that the theory of models succeeds in reinstating the doctrine of analogy in modern theological logic and in saving it from being a purely scholastic form of doctrine, and that analogy is to be interpreted in terms of a theory of models and not *vice versa*.

Are models descriptive?

We have been saying that one of the functions of models is to disclose reality, and that where several models are used in series, they are 'hinged' to a single reality. The question which I wish now to examine is whether we can legitimately ascribe the function of *description* to models.

Professor Ramsey rejects what he calls the 'deceptive attractions of descriptive language'[1] and it is very clear that his objection is to pictorial representations, which are thought to reflect reality with the accuracy of a mirror. Clearly he is not saying that when using model-language we are out of all relation to reality, or that the reality which is disclosed by the successful models is an undifferentiated blur. He does say, on the contrary, that models enable us 'to come to a reliable . . . understanding of the phenomena' and 'to be reliably articulate about (the universe)'.[2] The distinction between 'articulate' and 'describe' is one to which Professor Ramsey wishes to adhere very closely. Even although the former means 'to express clearly', he would interpret it rather as the delineation of relations within a mystery which might otherwise remain inexpres-

[1] *Op. cit.*, p. 68.   [2] *Op. cit.*, pp. 13ff.

sible. However, if we break with the equation of description with pictorial representation, then it becomes possible to include articulation within the meaning of description, and to say that articulation by means of models is the form which description takes when we are dealing with certain parts or aspects of reality. In fact, Professor Ramsey seems almost to prepare the way for this position when he allows[1] that 'the model arises in a moment of insight when the universe discloses itself in the points where the phenomena and the model meet'. The model is authenticated by reality. This admission is not a way of saying that there is a one-one correspondence between the model and reality. But it is to say that in employing created models we are describing reality in the only way that is possible to us.

When once again we give cash-value to our models, the position becomes clearer. When Jesus says, 'I am the shepherd', or 'I am the door', clearly he is not using language which is pictorially representative. Jesus did not go about Palestine leading sheep from place to place; nor did he protect the entrance to a house, and keep people out, or swinging back allow them to enter. At the same time, he was not, in using these models, failing to describe his own nature and function; nor did he imply that his nature was inexpressible, or his function indescribable. He was in fact describing his own nature and saying that he could be trusted as a leader through all the vicissitudes of life, and that he so loved his people that he would give his life for them. He was saying that it was his purpose to open the way for men to come to the father, and he invited men and women to enter God's presence through knowing him. When he said, 'This is my body which is broken for you', he was obviously not there and then breaking his own body; nor was he simply employing a metaphor which pointed beyond itself to an ineffable reality. He was speaking of his own death, and he was, by using this model, describing it as a sacrifice. So, too, when he says, 'This is my blood which is shed for the remission of the sins of many', he describes, by means of the model of the cup blessed and poured forth, the nature and meaning of his death. In other words, it is almost as if the model is compounded partly of an element which does not carry the ultimate reference to

[1] *Op. cit.*, pp. 13-14.

the reality disclosed, and partly of an element which has the direct reference to the reality and constitutes part of the disclosure. This latter element seems to be constituted of the area common to the two contexts whose intersection creates the metaphor situation.

Models and analogy

I should like to make two comments on the position we have now reached. The first is that we have returned again to the case for relating models to analogy—not, as we said, to a scholastic and quasi-mathematical form, but to one which does greater justice to the idiosyncrasies of human language as it is used, more justice that is to literary forms than to logical structures. Susan Stebbing[1] quotes a distinction drawn by J. M. Keynes between what he calls positive analogy and negative analogy. Given two entities S and N which resemble each other in definable respects which may be enumerated, thus, $p_1, p_2, p_3 \ldots p_n$ and differ from each other in further definable respects, thus, $r_1, r_2, r_3 \ldots r_n$; we denote the former the positive analogy and the latter the negative analogy. Clearly every analogy we employ consists of a balance of the one against the other. Or we may change the figure (or the analogy!) and say that between them they constitute a spectrum; and when the negative analogy far exceeds the positive we begin to approach the fanciful in literary description, or typological exegesis, or sermon illustration; and when the positive analogy far exceeds the negative, we are approximating to flat description. Proper analogy occurs in the middle range of the spectrum.

If I may digress for a moment: the balance of the negative to the positive analogy in ordinary conversational-analogical argument or illustration is one of the greatest sources both of misunderstanding and of the popular conversational sport of one-upmanship. When we ourselves employ any analogy, we do so because of the positive content which illustrates our point or our theme; but our opponents, with churlish malevolence, at once seize upon the negative analogy and demonstrate its plain absurdity. The two-upmanship reply at that point is: 'Of course, it is only an analogy', which reply is calculated to give you

[1] *A Modern Introduction to Logic*, Methuen 1933.

sufficient time to abandon that particular analogy and look for another more satisfactory.

Where, however, there is a heavy balance in favour of the negative analogy over the positive, it is not unusual for the speaker or the writer to quote several analogies one after another, so that collectively by throwing light upon one another and enriching one another they may establish the clearly significant positive analogy. In this process, the analogies, as it were, refine and define one another; they provide the means for determining their own accuracy; and among them, they yield the very disclosure of which Professor Ramsey spoke. But in doing so they describe through their progressively clarified positive analogy the reality to which they refer.

In Christology, generally, and in the biblical statements about Jesus Christ, we have both kinds of analogy—those which carry a fairly even balance between the negative and the positive analogy and those which show a preponderance of negative over positive analogy and which are offered, therefore, in rapid series. Examples of the first I would find in the several ways in which the Bible and subsequent soteriology have spoken of the death of Christ—as victory over evil powers and principalities, as ransom, as penal substitution, as vicarious satisfaction, as moral example, and so on. Here there is not the intensive interpenetration of one model by the other which we get in the second form; indeed, the history of soteriology shows how effectively one theory of the death of Christ can be formulated to the exclusion of the others. The parable of the wicked husbandmen in Luke 20.9-19 would be another case of an analogy whose balance of positive to negative is so even that no supporting analogies are required for the further definition of its meaning or its reference. The rapid succession type of analogy occurs in the Gospels, in the instance we have mentioned of the parables of the kingdom. Perhaps the best modern example is Hymn 419 in the *Revised Church Hymnary*, where the name of Jesus is spoken of, at one and the same time, as sounding sweet in a believer's ear, soothing his sorrows, healing his wounds, driving away his fear, calming the troubled breast; and finally, as being 'manna to the hungry soul, and to the weary rest'. The culmination comes when Jesus is addressed as 'Shepherd, Husband, Friend';

'Prophet, Priest and King'; 'Lord, Life, Way and End'. This plethora of models, of course, creates an almost infinite richness in the final description, as each helps the other in the process of greater definition.

What must be carefully emphasized, however, is that at no point is it quite possible to extract the positive analogy and to state it in a non-analogical way; or, if that view seems to be an overstatement, the end-product is such a two-dimensional, superficial account that it cannot compete with the analogies even as a description. It may have been some consideration of the sort which prompted the now famous line of Tillich that with the exception of the statement about Being Itself, all language about God is analogical. This difficulty, namely of transcending the model, the metaphor, or the analogy, prevents us from ever assuming that we have exhaustively described or defined the mystery of the Word made flesh. We never grasp it in the immediacy of non-analogical language.

Models as media of apprehension

The second general comment I have to make on the idea that model language is to be regarded as nonetheless descriptive may be illustrated from a theory which the late Professor Kemp Smith used to hold about the ontological status of secondary qualities. He was not prepared to say with the naive realists that they were externally existent in reality, that the things of the world were blue or green, cold or hot, sweet or sour, and so on, in themselves. Nor would he agree with the subjective idealists that these secondary qualities were purely subjective ideas, existing only in our minds and in no way related to anything that might be termed an external world. Between these two extremes, he argued, lay a more accurate view, that secondary qualities were the terms in which we apprehended the external world and consequently described it. He did not deny that the secondary qualities had an existence in their own right; they were events in a spatio-temporal continuum, complex occurrences with biochemical and physiological as well as physical aspects. But when their position is considered within the knower-known relationship, they function as the media through which reality is known by sense-percipient people, the form in which they understand reality and the means by which they adjust themselves to it, and indeed live their lives within it. The status of models in christology, we are contending, is somewhat similar. These are the terms in which we apprehend the person of Jesus Christ, or rather it is in such terms that he apprehends us—as the shepherd who leads us, cares for us and finally dies for us; as the door, through whom in very fact we enter into the presence of God; or as the way, in which to walk is to live life to its fulness. When, therefore, we use the models, we are not simply connecting one set of symbols by comparison with another, as if the reality to which they applied had no control over them. We are in fact talking about Christ, and we are *describing* him in terms of the models. We are saying that he is like this and this and this; and we check the models by what we have come to know about him. In the end of the day, then, our models are controlled and indeed authenticated by the reality, Christ, whom we have come to know albeit through them.

I should like at this point to make certain comments. The illustration from Kemp Smith's epistemology is not applicable in all respects to the christological model. Once again, we are using models as models! No one but a naive realist in epistemology would want to say nowadays that if we were to probe scientifically into the microcosms of reality they would bear the qualities which reality reveals at the macrocosmic level. Colours, tastes, smells, heat, cold, pressure, sounds disappear among waves or vibrations or electrical charges or discharges; and scientists and even some philosophers may be forgiven for thinking the latter to be reality and the former illusion. What we must admit, however, is that reality may not 'in itself' have many of the characteristics which sense perception attributes to it. It would, I should say, be unthinkable that Christ 'in himself' should not possess in some measure at least some of the qualities which we attribute to him when we describe him in terms of the models, say, which we derive from the Bible. Not only would we want to hold that there does not exist the disparity between the models (partly in the positive analogy of their content and structure) and the character of Christ which distinguishes sense-data from waves and vibrations; but we shall insist that there can be no contradiction by the mystery still

68

remaining within the person of Jesus Christ and his nature as we understand it through the models. Mystery surrounding Christ there must always be, but it is not the sort of mystery which might turn out to be a denial of what we know of Christ when we speak of him as shepherd, or ransom or door.

Secondly, we are now coming very close to the point of recognizing that some of the language which we use of Christ has finally transcended the status of model to become immediately descriptive of Christ. I feel a good deal of sympathy with Tillich's view that Being Itself is ascribed to God non-analogically. It is difficult to see how such a term could be employed analogically; it seems to have a divine set from the very start. But some of the terms which we have come to apply to Christ, chiefly on the basis of their scriptural origin, come into the same category; for example, when we speak of him as life, truth, and logos, it is extremely difficult to cast these attributes in a negative-positive form so common to analogical predication. There is an identity of content between them and the very nature of Christ which precludes the rough approximations of model-type assertions. To say so is not to deny either that when Christ first used these terms of himself or was so described by St John the Evangelist, there was then an element of analogy in them; or that we may use these terms today in reference to other realities than Christ. What is meant is that now we know that Christ is the key to what these terms signify, for he is each one, and that other applications are declensions from that absolute meaning, secondary and derivative applications.

The position for which I am arguing, then, is this, that the terms in which we understand Christ's character are the ways in which in fact he exists. We reject the theory that the models are simply ideal or mental representations of a reality which may differ from them, as we reject the theory that like signposts they point to a reality which bears no more than a directional relation to them: the signpost with the name New York 50 miles tells you nothing about the character, size, climate, of the city except that it lies so far in a certain direction. If we speak of Christ as a shepherd it is because he has certain qualities which authenticate the comparison, and it is of those qualities themselves that we are talking when we describe him as shepherd.

Without such earthing of our language in the person of Jesus Christ, it is hard to see what such language is about.

The normative role of models

A further characteristic or function of models in christology is that they may become *normative*; that is, they tend to be the criteria by which we judge the truth or falsity of the statements about Jesus Christ. Probably they have always fulfilled this function from the earliest days of Christian theology. When models such as the notion of the Messiah, or the Son of man, with all their rich associations ousted such notions as that of prophet or rabbi or magic-worker, a criterion—norms—had been set up to regulate and control the correct description of Jesus Christ and to condemn the inaccurate, which eventually became known as the heretical. The position became still more acute in the great period of the christological controversies when the models which the various parties adopted guided them in their own assertions and in their condemnation of one another. Traditionally, however, the Church has come to rely not upon models as the norms of its theology but upon creeds. Even at the time of the Reformation, when the doctrine and practice of the medieval Church was laid alongside the written word of God and tested by its faithfulness to that word; and when the written word of God as witnessed to by the *testimonium internum spiritus sancti* was acknowledged to be the supreme rule of faith; there very soon came a time when men formulated confessions to secure the right interpretation of scripture and to prepare young people by catechesis to ensure a correct understanding by them of the open Bible placed in their hands.

It always seemed to me a curious anomaly of our celebration in 1960 of the quatercentenary of the Reformation that we should have made so much of the rediscovery of the Bible and so little of our desperate need for subordinate standards. It was right that we should honour the former of these Reformation achievements; for the theology of at least the past two decades has been more closely related to biblical foundation than probably any since the days of the Reformation itself. These have been the great decades of biblical theology, of the biblical doctrine of man, of time, of baptism, and so on. But at the same time we are becoming fully aware of what I can only call the intellectual dishonesty of the Articles Declaratory and the Declaratory Acts, which over the years have allowed ministers of the churches in Scotland to withhold their confessional allegiance to those elements in the Westminster *Confession of Faith* which do not belong to the substance of the faith. I refuse to believe that one may excerpt from the Westminster Confession the doctrine of double predestination or the view of hell, and leave the other doctrines of the documents unaffected. To remove double predestination is to propose a change in the understanding of the character of God. To alter the character of Sunday from that assumed in the Confession to something of a more liberal nature, as has been suggested by the General Assembly of the Church of Scotland in recent years, is to change also the pattern of life as the Westminster divines conceived it. There is a grave vacuum in Reformed theology which was originally filled by the classical confessions, of which the *Scots Confession* was among the most outstanding, and later by the Westminster Confession, and which has been created by the inroads of continuing theological reform. This vacuum cannot be readily filled by wide use of the primary standard of doctrine and theology, namely the scriptures; for they all too clearly are interpreted this way or that, if one may not be unduly cynical, according to doctrinal, confessional or ecclesiastical preference.

It is at this very point that models have acquired a normative importance which they have not hitherto had on their own. Previously, they may have operated normatively, but they have done so within the framework or under the cover of an accepted subordinate standard—a creed, a confession or a rule of faith. When L. S. Thornton uses A. N. Whitehead's category of 'organism' as the central interpretative principle for expounding the person of Jesus Christ, he is not simply adopting a concept which is hermeneutically useful and intellectually contemporary. He has adopted a norm which permits him to make certain christological statements and prevents him from making others. A line is now drawn between the true and the false, the valid and the invalid. When the kenoticists adopted the notion of *kenosis*, they were not simply constructing a christology on the basis of a text in St Paul (Phil. 2.5ff.). They were adopting a model on the basis of which they accepted some traditional christological statements and departed from others. They made a great deal of those christological passages which emphasized the weakness, the hunger, the humanity of Christ, but minimized any which appeared to make too much of his retention upon earth of the full attributes of deity, those which he had before the incarnation and which he would recover thereafter. Nor need the model be normative solely for christology. Kenoticism can easily extend its model into the ethical field and interpret the christological norm as a behavioural norm. The revival of the Chalcedonian two-nature model in christology has been very rapidly followed by its penetration into other fields—the doctrine of the Church and the doctrine of the Bible, for example—and it has produced its own crop of charges of heresy against those positions from which it differed, as it did in the fifth century. We have heard of an Eutychean doctrine of the Church, or a Nestorian doctrine of the scriptures; and the use of the adjectives derived from the names of christological heresies is its own evidence of the powerfully normative functions of models in modern christology and theology.

This normative function of models may explain two rather paradoxically incongruous aspects of this modern scene. The first is the emotive element which is not far-removed from many theological controversies. The *odium theologicum* has never been something to joke about: it has cast a shadow over a subject which should throughout have been irradiated solely by the grace and love of Almighty God. But it has inevitably arisen where, using their models as heresy-detectors, theologians have thought to discredit one another's views by aligning them with ancient falsehoods. There is an unfortunate custom intruding into the modern christological scene, of naming one's opponent, of identifying his views with those of some dishonoured heretic. Quite apart from the anachronism which often lies at the heart of such judgments, the effect upon the atmosphere in which theological discussion is conducted is disastrous. Truth, least of all theological truth, never came through hatred, least of all through the *odium theologicum*. The second aspect of the modern scene, which is connected with the normative character of models is the way in which, as a result of the collapse of the subordinate standards above-mentioned—the Thirty-nine Articles have suffered as badly in this respect as the Westminster Confession or the Sermons of Wesley—the different churches have come to acknowledge together the validity for them all of agreed models. Whereas, in the past, the subordinate standards which operated radically to divide denominations; in the present situation, models which surmount the old barriers create a basis for ecumenical unity. The point is often put in a different way, of course, when it is said that church differences are now horizontal rather than vertical, and that the same kinds of theological differences reproduce themselves almost exactly within the different denominations. This ecumenical influence of the models in their normative capacity may, in part, atone for the part they play in fostering the *odium theologicum* within denominations. The unfortunate aspect of the situation is that both consequences follow from a single cause.

The integrative function of models

Closely allied to the previous function of models in christology is one which I have called their *integrative* function. By their presence in christological formulation, they provide it with a unity which it did not have when theologians did not rely so heavily as they do today on models as controlling categories. At one time, the contents of theology were presented as if they constituted the several atomic items of a series, a longer version of the Apostle's Creed, with no internal coherence and no genuinely systematic structure. The fashion nowadays is the reverse: theology is highly integrated and carefully structured, and the medium of articulation is the theological model. This end is achieved in somewhat different ways perhaps in different areas of scholarship.

For example, in the field of biblical studies there has been a revival of interest in typological forms of exegesis. Sometimes typology has taken the straightforward action of discerning the lineaments of Christ in Old Testament situations, as when it is suggested that Jacob wrestled with Christ at Peniel,[1] so that the imposition has been of New Testament concepts upon Old Testament situations, characters and events. Nor can we ever forget

[1] Gen. 32.24ff.

that it was not left to patristic, reformed or neo-orthodox expositors to invent the practice of typology. For Christians it is already embodied in scripture, in St Paul's affirmation[1] that the spiritual Rock of which the Israelites drank in the wilderness and which had followed them in their journeying was Christ; and clearly in St Paul it was no newly created art. He was adopting an accepted form of Jewish exegesis. At other times, the typology operates in a directly opposite direction, and the Old Testament provides the *typos* for the exposition of New Testament situations and occurrences. A notable example of this kind of typology is given by John Marsh in his *The Fulness of Time*[2] where the pattern of the Exodus is used as the basis for the exposition of the life and ministry of Jesus Christ. Again, it may be a concept such as that of covenant which spans the Old Testament and the New which provides the over-all *typos* for the exposition of the central themes of both Testaments. In such a case it is difficult to determine the direction of the flow of interpretation. Another type which seems to span and include both the Old Testament and the New is that used so frequently in the sermons in the Acts of the Apostles, namely, promise and fulfilment. An interesting extension of the biblical type-form is to be seen in the way in which Barth uses the parables of the prodigal son, and the notion of 'the far country' to describe the distance which God in Christ came to redeem mankind. These examples are chosen wildly and at random; for I am not so much concerned with the variety of typological exegesis and interpretation as with the fact that typology is an instance of the integrative function which models fulfil, more particularly in the field of biblical studies. Its employment in this field raises constantly the question of the point at which the type, applied to the text, begins to distort and misrepresent, and to violate the canons of historiography and of historicity which are implicit in the biblical narrative.

The unity of the Bible itself a model

When we speak of the *integrative* function of the models employed in biblical typology, it is not always observed that the very notion of an integrative function is, in a sense, itself a

---

[1] I Cor. 10.4.   [2] Nisbet 1952, pp. 44ff., 84ff.

model. To put the matter in another way: most typologies, whether ancient or modern, presuppose the *unity* of the Bible. But the very notion of unity is itself a model. Perhaps someone might be tempted to say that it is a purely formal model, but when the evidence is examined it would appear that it is the structure of the unity model which in most cases determines the form which the typology takes and the lengths to which it is prepared to go. I should like, therefore, to spend a little time in consideration of what the unity of the Bible is thought to be, for our conception of the unity of the Bible, or the form of the model of unity which we employ, prescribes to a very considerable degree the way in which we use not only the Old Testament but also the New when speaking of Jesus Christ.

The obvious first conception of unity which springs to mind is that associated with the old Protestant view of the Bible. It is a unity of system, a unity of propositions which all directly or allegorically or typologically refer to Jesus Christ; but recourse was had to allegory and type only after it had proved absolutely impossible to make the direct reference. The consequence was that texts from the Old Testament almost as readily as from the New could be applied to Christ. It is as if Christ were contemporaneous with all parts of the scriptures, whether before or after his birth. A sustained passage such as Isa. 52.13-53.12, still constitutes a major problem for Old Testament scholars, if pressed to say of *whom* in fact the author was speaking when describing the servant of Yahweh—an actual known figure of the day, who had suffered greatly; the whole nation of Israel in their historical sufferings; the ideal Israel, as it would be were it truly to be God's servant and God's agent in the world; the loyal and faithful core of Israel, the minority who were to suffer for the nation; or indeed the messiah that was yet to come. But on the view of the unity of the Bible now before us the passage is an accurate description of the person of Jesus Christ. It found concrete and final embodiment in him.

It has become customary nowadays to be explicit in rejection of the so-called proof-text method, the type of theology which resorts constantly to scriptural quotations in order to clinch a point in theological controversy. The determination of the relation between the quotation and what it is thought to prove can be an exceedingly complex exercise in hermeneutics. Not infrequently is the text designed to conceal some lacuna or *non sequitur* in the main argument. Often it is assumed that what the text is taken to prove is a paraphrase of the text itself. The presence of a textual reference, particularly when inserted within brackets, should be taken as a danger signal by anyone engaged in the serious reading of theology. The content of the text apart from the bracket is to be approached with the greatest caution, and the brackets themselves to be entered at walking speed. But if you succeed in discovering the relation between what a man puts within the brackets and what he says or writes outside of them you will have discovered the secret springs of his theology.

Unity of devotional purpose

Though it does not come in quite the correct logical order, I should like to mention as the next form which the model of unity may take, unity of devotional purpose. It comes at this point, however, only because it forms an interesting subsection to our notion of unity of system. For while perhaps a considerable number of us might reject the idea that the Bible is a system of propositions contemporary with Christ, as one of our theological principles; nevertheless, our devotional practice would imply a rather different position. When we join with the whole church on Good Friday to listen to Isa. 52.13-53.12; when we hear once again the story of Abraham and Isaac,[1] and particularly the words of Abraham, 'My son, God will provide himself a lamb for a burnt offering'; or when we read the 23rd Psalm or Isa. 9.6f.; it is inevitable that we should at once be thinking of Christ in the terms of each of those passages. When the reference is not so clearly to the person of Christ, but more to some aspect of his character or some event in his life, we may still make the application even though we are well aware that the original author was speaking about someone in his own time and not about Christ, who may have lived as many as eight hundred years later. There is an extension of this process into the ethical field when we find that a command given in a context quite foreign to us, a command given even in a passage

[1] Gen. 22.3ff.

76

whose authenticity we might on textual critical grounds feel compelled to question, comes to us as a direct imperative of the word of God. Those are all everyday experiences for those who use the Bible as the basis for the daily devotional period. Their significance is that the Bible is clearly acknowledged by us to have a unity of devotional purpose not dissimilar to the kind of unity which we called systematic, and which many people would reject as part of their theological principles. To put the case quite bluntly, they reject fundamentalism as a theological formula only to accept it as a devotional presupposition. I sometimes wonder whether it is not in this area that we ought to be looking for the cause of the breakdown of the devotional disciplines of our time not only among the people of the Church but also among ministers. It would be too extreme to say that to fail to correlate devotional reflection with textual or theological criticism and analysis is to base one's devotions upon a lie and to be a hypocrite; but doubt about the historicity of an incident, or the authenticity of a saying may prevent either from being the medium of the word of God to us in our need. It certainly would seem to be the case that it is the fundamental sense of the unity of devotional purpose of the Bible which sustains the more strictly theological conviction about its systematic propositional unity.

Unity of centre

To return to the theological analysis of the model of unity, we may mention as the third form—unity of centre. This model may be looked at in two ways. On the one hand we may think of the unity which is given to the circumference of a circle through the relation in which it stands to its centre. The Bible may then be thought of as the circumference of a circle with radii pointing inwards to Christ as its centre. On this view, the Bible is eccentric: it has a centre beyond itself. To understand the Bible we have to look in the direction in which it is pointing and wherever we open it, we find that it points to the same person, Jesus Christ. We do not find that every radius points in the same direction, for the simple reason that every radius begins from a different point on the circumference. The starting-points of Abraham and Moses, of Amos and Isaiah, of Peter and John, of Paul and James, were all different, but at the centre of the circle on the circumference of which they stood was Christ himself. Without him they would not have existed as a circle; with him at the centre they are bound to one another. On the other hand, we may think of Christ creating of the Bible a unity, by standing between them as the one to whom the Old Testament looks forward and the New Testament looks back. The former utters the promise of the One that is yet to come; the other declares the fulfilment of the promise, proclaiming that that One has come. Consequently, the relation of Christ to the Old Testament is different from that which he bears to the New. It is impossible then to adopt the position of those who hold to a unity of system and to relate all of scripture uniformly to Christ. Instead, it is as if they were a gulf between the two, a gulf created by the Incarnation. Prophecy looking towards Christ can never be used of him as if it knew that he had come. Expectation is misrepresented if it is merged with consummation. They stand separated but in their separation held together as the two ultimate parts of the context of the Incarnation, its before and after.

Unity in the records of God's mighty acts

It would be wrong to omit from a review of this kind some reference to the model of unity which conceives of it as a record of God's mighty acts. This form is perhaps ultimately a combination of unity of centre and unity of system. It shares with the former the fact that it is eccentrically constituted; it is a record of acts done by God; it points beyond itself to the events which it records. On the other hand, it forms a very closely knit system of interrelationships, in which the divine purpose unfolds itself to the redemption of mankind. Operating with this model christologically, we see the Incarnation as the supreme mighty act of God, the consummation of all else. With this model, the method of christology tends to be dogmatic-historical. But once again, the point emerges that the model defines and controls the method.

Criteria governing the use of models in christology

At the start I mentioned that one of the most characteristic features of christology is the immense range of terms which the Church has employed to deploy its account of Jesus Christ. Of those that are drawn from the Old Testament some are applied directly to Jesus; while others, given a special significance in being applied to Jesus, in the process are deeply changed. Yet others are New Testament terms *simpliciter* and they derive their meaning strictly from within its limits. But the history of christology has yielded a whole new crop of fresh terms, their originals coming from philosophy, ethics, social or economic circumstances, or even biology. When we look at this immense range, we cannot easily escape the question of how these different models gain ascendancy and popularity the one over the other. Few criteria would seem to operate.

The first is that the model which correlates a higher proportion of the biblical material concerning Christ and of the church's witness to Christ and obedience to him, than does its fellows is the more likely to gain allegiance. To adopt Professor Ramsey's language: it is isomorphic with a greater number of biblical and church phenomenal situations than are competing models and consequently is the medium of disclosure over a wider area than they are. For example, the model of the *eschaton*, while referring primarily to the end-time in history, has in recent years been related not only to the whole Incarnation, in terms of what we now call realized eschatology, but also to individual incidents and events within the Incarnation itself. Some of Jesus' parables are seen to have an eschatological significance; baptism is linked with the *eschaton*; the Last Supper points forward both to the coming crucifixion and to the end of history. An isomorphic structure, paradigmatically instanced in the *eschaton* proper, links together a whole range of phenomena, and discloses the presence of him who is not *eschaton* but *eschatos*. The covenant model we have already seen plays the same correlating role, linking the death of Christ not only to the Old Testament and God's purposes of salvation there declared, but to the Last Supper and to every celebration of the sacrament of the Lord's Supper which takes place thereafter in the Church. Other comprehensive models of this standard come to mind— of the kingdom of heaven or the Son of man in the Gospels, the model of stewardship in the letters of the apostle Paul, the Lamb of the book of the Revelation, and so on. Any one of these models correlates an immense variety of biblical material. By comparison, at the other extreme, we might quote the model of 'husband' which appears in John Newton's hymn, 'How sweet the name of Jesus sounds'.[1] This model would have a much narrower range of relevance than some of the other models which appear in the same line, 'Shepherd, Friend, King', and so on.

The second criterion which seems to apply in the selection of models, almost one might say in their self-selection for it is not always a procedure which is explicitly and consciously followed by the Church, is as follows. The model which sets the phenomena of scripture and of the life of faith in the Church based upon scripture within the deepest perspective tends to gain ascendancy. The model of the Logos which places Jesus Christ in the context of the ultimate nature of God, which locates him within the very being of God from the beginning; which sees the events of the incarnation as the final consummation of a process which had been taking place throughout the whole history of Israel; a model with such depth to it is superior to one such as rabbi, which pictures Christ only as a teacher, a creature of time, coming to be and passing away. The model of the Son of God gives the same depth of perspective as does that of the Logos, and it established itself over against some such notion as that of wonder-worker, which makes him a person only of his own age and of human stature. Probably the ultimate ground for our rejection of a purely human Jesus is the shallowness of the presentation it offers to us, and the resultant sense of loss and disappointment that it creates within us. It has omitted an entire dimension. He takes a two-dimensional approach to a reality which has depth and mystery to it. Its picture is flat where the reality is perspectival.

The third criterion we might consider to be relevant when comparing christological models is that that model is preferable which throws light on those areas of our religious thought and action to which we should have felt it to be immediately relevant. The notion of the *eschaton* is concerned with the end of history, and with that anticipation of the end which took place

[1] *Revised Church Hymnary*, Hymn 419.

in the incarnation and has yielded the notion of eschatology. But it has a relevance beyond the interpretation of history, the parables and even the sacraments, to the field of ethics. If Jesus Christ is the great contemporaneous *eschatos*, then we are living now as in the very end-time; we stand now under God's mercy and judgment; so that we dare not live our lives carelessly and thoughtlessly or sinfully. The Judge and Saviour awaits. Morality in these terms acquires an urgency and gravity which it would not have on other historical or metaphysical grounds. The Son of Man model, even although and perhaps because it is such an exceedingly difficult model to plot with accuracy, has fruitful and illuminating points of contact with the Christian doctrine of man: a model primarily applied to Jesus is a most useful basis of exposition of further aspects of the humanity which he bore. Stewardship, a model drawn from an agrarian economy, by a rather remarkable transvaluation, is an effective medium of demonstrating not only our obligations to God and our neighbour in respect of time spent, talents employed and possessions shared, but also the very grace of God towards us and our effective guardianship and propagation of the Gospel which is the story of his grace towards us. An effective model illumines areas to which it was not in the first place directed.

So, fourthly, the models which finally establish themselves in the Church's understanding of the scriptures and in its proclamation of the Gospel, are those which mediate Christ, his love, his forgiveness, his power and his truth; which sustain faith and renew it with the very life of Christ; which lead to fresh commitment to him for work to be done in his name and for his kingdom's sake; and which issue in sincere obedience to Christ and to his will. The model which does not meet these empirical demands, however impeccably demonstrated its scriptural authenticity, however dogmatically respectable its sources, can never hope to survive as a genuine medium of insight into Christ's nature and of our obedient and loving response to him. In a word, the only genuine purpose of a christological model is to make possible the service and love of Christ, through a true understanding of him.

4

THE TWO-NATURE MODEL

SYNOPSIS

The two-nature model has the following features:

The description of Jesus Christ as both human and divine, but (a) the scriptures do not think of Jesus in dualistic terms: he moves among men as one person. (b) Nevertheless there is a *prima facie* case for the two-nature theory even in the scriptures. In the actual execution of its task, the two-nature model drew heavily upon the logic of Aristotle's *Categoriae* c. 5. 'Substance in the primary sense (*prōtē ousia*) is that which is neither predicated of a subject nor exists in a subject (i.e. it is a particular man or horse).' 'Secondary substances (*deuterai ousiai*) are things (species, genus or universal) to which the things (primary substances) belong.' The two-nature model (*una hypostasis* and *duo physeis*) virtually identifies *hypostasis* with *prōtē ousia* and *physis* with *deutera ousia*.

The key to the understanding of the several forms of the two-nature model is the principle of 'no *physis* without an *hypostasis*' or 'no *physis anhypostatos*'. This principle apparently ignored in the *anhypostasia* of the Chalcedonian definition is acknowledged in:

1. Nestorianism.
2. Eutycheanism.
3. The *enhypostasia* of Leontius of Byzantium; though in the latter it seems to have entailed a type of Apollinarianism (cf. K. Barth, IV/2, pp. 49f.).
4. The *synthetos hē hypostasis* theory of Ephraim of Antioch.

The two-nature model comes under severe criticism at several points today: (a) its notion of substance; (b) its conception of human nature as a static definition; cf. contemporary views of human nature —e.g. of Jean-Paul Sartre, K. Barth (III/1, pp. 184ff.).

The Two-Nature Model

IT WILL have become clear by now that in a quite fundamental way the model is the controlling element in the development of any discipline. It determines how we shall handle the given from which the discipline takes its beginning. It dictates the method we follow in imposing form and structure upon the given. It regulates our discussions with one another upon the validity or invalidity of statements made within the given. I propose in the second half of our discussion to examine more closely some three of the more important models which have in the past operated in the christological field, and more particularly to try to discover to what extent they continue to be models that we may rightly employ in the execution of our christological task.

Jesus Christ, human and divine: the biblical witness

Beginning with the two-nature model I should like to indicate its main constituent features. The feature that is most obvious is, of course, the description of the person of Jesus Christ as both human and divine. We have become so accustomed to this sort of characterization that we are unaware now that even using this quite simple descriptive form we have firmed into hard usage something that was still fluid and malleable in the scriptures themselves, and we have even given the description a twist which is not immediately recognizable as biblical.

The scriptures obviously do not think of Jesus Christ in dualistic terms, which in honesty we must admit is one of the first impressions created by the use of the two-nature model. Jesus moves among men and walks and talks as a single person, even in situations which later theology has come to associate with one nature rather than with the other. When Luke says at 2.52 that 'Jesus increased in wisdom and stature, and in favour with God and man' neither does he say that it was in respect of his human nature that he was developing from childhood to maturity nor does he even raise the question of how this growth could be related to a perfect divine nature. There was a single, not a dual, situation, with the boy Jesus becoming a man. When he worked his miracles, feeding the five thousand,[1] healing the woman[2] 'which had a spirit of infirmity eighteen years', when he cured the blind man,[3] no suggestion is made by the evangelists that these were particularly a demonstration of his divine powers or nature. Even in the great prayer of John 17, when Jesus makes unmistakably plain his awareness of his oneness with the father,[4] there is not the slightest hint that one part of his person is speaking, or that what he is saying might not be entirely true of the whole of his person. When he faces the final agonies on Calvary, no excuse is offered for his weakness, for example, that it is in his human nature that he is brought low, while his divine nature still reigns in heaven. It was left to later apologetic to invent subtleties, one might even say deceptions, of this sort. After the resurrection, in spite of the quasi-incorporeal character of his manifestations, Jesus is presented as having a body; he still bears the wound marks in his side and hands, into which a doubting Thomas may thrust his hand and his fingers to obtain what we would call empirical evidence. But it is evidence not simply that the body of Christ has not been annihilated by death and that his human nature is raised from the dead, but also that, as we would say, the divine nature, that Word that was with God in the beginning, the Word that was made flesh, had been brought back from the dead. The implication is clear: the indicator to the presence of the human nature operates automatically as the marker for the divine nature, so completely are they regarded as elements in a single situation. The matter of one being present with the other is not even mentioned: it is taken for granted.

It would be wrong, however, to give the impression that the human-divine categorization is an improper imposition which later theology made upon an originally basically simple biblical given. There must be some justification both in the words and the events recorded in scripture to give the categorization a *prima facie* plausibility. It is to be found, as shown by the example we gave, in some of the things Jesus did according to the narratives, for reflective men pondering over the events after

[1] Luke 9.14ff.   [2] Luke 13.11ff.   [3] John 9.1ff.   [4] John 17.5, 10, 21.

the resurrection must have seen that even his moments of greatest human weakness were accompanied by a courage and glory which were more than human; that even when he worked his miracles, most of all when he was raised from the dead, the situations had a human side which was an inalienable aspect of them. So often it was human compassion that was the motive of the miracles; it was the presence of the human body which carried conviction about the reality of the resurrection. In other words, the distinction arose out of the given for anyone who pondered it, in the Holy Spirit. The distinction, one might then conclude, was implicit in the given which confronted the disciples and the evangelists, were it not that we must say that it was to some extent explicit in some of the ways men spoke of Jesus. The Son of God concept may be and has been taken as a recognition of the divine nature of Jesus; and the Son of man concept in addition to its apocalyptic associations, has been said to carry the human reference.

> But we must guard against ascribing also to the first Christians —much less to Jesus himself—the intention of using the Son of God designation to say something about the Son's identity of substance with the Father. The New Testament title does point to Christ's coming from the Father and his deity, but not in the sense of later discussions about 'substance' and 'natures'.[1]

The birth narratives in Luke's Gospel, whether we decide on their ultimate historical authenticity or not, clearly indicate that from a very early date the Church acknowledged in Jesus a person who for all his being born of Mary has a mysterious, divine beginning described by saying that he was conceived by the Holy Ghost. The sustained witness to what we call the deity of Christ in the aforementioned Great Prayer of John 17 combines in that Gospel with countless testimonies to the genuine reality of the humanity of Christ. The basic material is all there in scripture for the Church's subsequent definition of a firm distinction between the human nature of Jesus Christ and the divine; but scripture prefers not to speak of the distinction in these terms. The change is not all gain, as may be seen from a

---

[1] Oscar Cullmann, *The Christology of the New Testament* (ET), SCM Press 1959, p. 270.

comparison of the colourful biblical descriptions with the often sterile, logical structures of subsequent scholasticism.

In fact had the point been put with any directness to, say, St John, whether he might not be persuaded to use the term divine, *theios* rather than *theos* (God) of Christ, his reply would have been that the former is much too equivocal. It threatens to place Christ in some intermediate status lower than God and higher than man, a *tertium quid* with identity with neither. 'The Word was with God', says the Prologue to St John's Gospel, 'and the Word was God'. To quote Hoskyns and Davey,[1]

> Since the anarthrous *Theos* is personal, more is stated than that the Word is divine. The Word of God is no neuter thing, no mere power: He acts with personal consciousness and will.

The New Testament method, then, is not to fix the description of Jesus Christ by means of a sharp dualism, but rather to elaborate the various situations in which Christ gave himself *to* men and women, and for them, to tell over again all the wonderful things he said, and how he opened up the very heart of God to believers. One circumstance, therefore, that we shall have to mark very carefully in our consideration of the two-nature model is the extent to which it succeeds in conserving the unity of the person of Jesus Christ.

The Aristotelian sources of the two-nature model

In the actual execution of its task the two-nature model in most of its forms draws heavily on the logic of Aristotle's *Categoriae* c.5. One of the relevant passages may be quoted[2] at length, for it deals with the very important distinction between primary substance (*prōtē ousia*) and secondary substance (*deutera ousia*).

> Substance in the most literal and primary and common sense of the term is that which is neither predicated of a subject nor exists in a subject, as for example, the individual man or horse. These things are called secondary substances to which, as species, belong the things called substances in the primary sense and also the

[1] *The Fourth Gospel*, Faber and Faber 1940, I, p. 136.
[2] 2a.11-19 translated by Walter and Martha Kneale, *The Development of Logic*, Oxford 1962, p. 26, a book to which I should like publicly to acknowledge my debt.

genera of these species. For example, the individual man belongs to the species man, and the genus of the species is animal. These, then, are called secondary substances as for example both man and animal.

It is important that we should endeavour to grasp what Aristotle is saying. The distinction he here makes becomes regulative, as we shall see, of the definition of orthodox theology some seven hundred years after he made it, and remained so, one might say, even until our time. Perhaps it is simplest to begin by breaking down this rather concentrated account into the form of an example, 'Tom Jones is human'. Here Tom Jones is the primary substance. Humanity is predicated of him, though admittedly the Greek structure would oblige us to say 'man' rather than 'humanity'. As we would put it, he is the subject of all the circumstances, characteristics, qualities and experiences that we would normally associate with being human, or occur within the range of being human. Tom Jones is cold; ambitious; friendly; married or industrious. He is the subject to whom we refer the different predicates we have mentioned in the sentence; the subject, not just in the grammatical sense, in which a subject is so-called in relation to the predicate of the sentence, but the actual subject who has these qualities, adopts certain attitudes or reaches certain decisions. So we can see why Aristotle has contended that primary substance in this sense 'is neither predicated of a subject nor exists in a subject'. We would not think of saying that Tom Jones could be predicated of anything or anyone else, or that he exists in anything or anyone else. He exists in his own right, very much Tom Jones. Secondary substance, on the other hand, is predicated of something else, and it must always exist in something else. Sometimes, the secondary substance is a very inclusive genus such as animal, or only a species such as man; but all primary substances belong to secondary substances, either genera or species.

In parenthesis, it ought to be pointed out that Aristotle seems to move rather too readily from talk about predication to talk about belonging to a species or genus, but this assumption has been so widely commented upon that it is perhaps sufficient here only to draw attention to it. Further, he equates 'being predicated of a subject' (*kata tinos legesthai*) with 'being in something' (*en tini einai*)—a point to which we shall later return. His main contention is fairly clear.

At *Categoriae* 5, (2a.34ff.)[1] Aristotle writes:

> Everything except primary substances is either predicable of primary substances or present in them as subjects. . . . Animal is predicated of man, and therefore of individual man; for if there were no individual man of whom it could be predicated, it could not be predicated of man at all. . . . Everything is either predicated of primary substances or present in them; and if these last did not exist, it would be impossible for anything else to exist.

Aristotle is understood here to be affirming one form of his theory of universals. While Plato argued that universals exist *ante res*—the Forms pre-exist the particulars which embody them; and nominalists much later argued that universals exist *post res*—we derive them conceptually from the world of existent things which are qualified by various attributes; Aristotle's position was that universals exist *in rebus*, that is, only as realized in particular subjects. If the world of ordinary existence were to disappear, Plato would still have his ideal Forms, laid up in heaven in perfection and the nominalists could still retain the concepts of real things in their minds; but for Aristotle with ordinary existence would disappear the universals also, 'for without primary substance, it would be impossible for anything else to exist'. Normally, also, that would be the direction of the argument: if there is no *prōtē ousia*, primary substance, there can be no secondary substance, *deutera ousia*.

No physis anhypostatos: *origins of the theorem*

These two principles which we have selected from the *Categoriae* of Aristotle became, in fact, the foundation of the two-nature model, subject to one qualification; namely, that for the distinction between *prōtē ousia* and *deutera ousia* was substituted that between *hypostasis* and *physis*. The theory of *universalia in rebus*, that the *deutera ousia* does not exist if there is no *prōtē ousia*, was employed in the form that there is no *physis* without an *hypostasis*, no *physis anhypostatos*. The ubiquity of this principle in post- and pre-Chalcedonian times is strongly emphasized by

---

[1] Again following the translation of W. and M. Kneale, *op. cit.*, p. 30.

R. V. Sellers (in *The Council of Chalcedon*[1]), who discovers it in John Maxentius, *Dial c. Nestorian* i.6, and Ephraim of Antioch in Photius, Biblioth. Cod. ccxxix. P.G. ciii.993C; and it could be added that it is implied in the christology of Hippolytus[2] in so far as he anticipates the doctrine of *enhypostasia*. Timothy, Bishop of Alexandria, could write in *Refutation of the Synod of Chalcedon and the Tome of Leo*, Pt. 6: 'There is no nature which has not its *hypostasis*, and there is no *hypostasis* which exists without its *prosōpon*'; and Philoxenus in *Against Nestorius*[3]: 'There is no nature (*k'yânâ*) without a person (*q'nômâ*) neither is a person without a nature.'

In our next sections the determinative influence of this single principle of no *physis* without an *hypostasis* upon all shades of christological thought in the formative centuries of that discipline, as well as in modern times, will be illustrated. For the moment it may be important to pause to notice what is happening. In the New Testament, as we saw, there is the acknowledgment, the confession of Jesus Christ as both human and divine, a distinction drawn in a variety of terms but nevertheless fundamental to the Church's understanding of Christ's person. This distinction is about to be expressed in a model whose basic structural features are drawn from the heart of Aristotle's logic. This fact has to be kept clearly before us, because in many of the christological controversies, biblical texts seem to be so constantly the subject of difference of opinion, that one might be pardoned for thinking that these great controversies dealt only with matters of biblical exegesis. On the contrary, it could fairly be said that it was this 'no *physis anhypostatos*' principle which was the great divider and it is the clue to the variety of biblical exegesis. The quite astonishing further fact about this principle is that whereas it seems to us to have a fairly straightforward connotation, when applied to the christological material it permits of a whole range of christological interpretations. This range is our immediate next concern.

No physis anhypostatos: *in Nestorianism*

In selecting a number of representative positions in illustra-

---

[1] SPCK 1953, p. 318 n. 2 and p. 188.   [2] *c. Noetum* 15.
[3] Both Timothy and Philoxenus are quoted by R. V. Sellers, *op. cit.*, pp. 260 and 260 n. 4.

tion of how the 'no *physis anhypostatos*' principle was used in the classical period of controversy (fourth and fifth centuries) I do not wish to become involved in too much critical detail, discussing, for example, whether Nestorius was a Nestorian and so on. It will serve our purpose if we are able to show how this principle might be embodied in a specific model, even though there is doubt as to the authenticity of the writings or traditional interpretation of an author's thought.

Perhaps the most obvious implementation of the principle is to be found generally in what is known as the school of Antioch, and associated, when falling into heretical form, with the name of Nestorius. Given that Jesus Christ is to be regarded as both human and divine, and that there is 'no *physis* without an *hypostasis*', it would seem to follow that in Jesus Christ there are two *physeis* and two *hypostaseis*. This contention is reinforced both by Greek philosophical views about the difference between God who is impassible, incorruptible and eternal and man who is passible, corruptible and mortal, and by biblical accounts of the ways in which God surpasses man, for example, according to Isa. 55.8f.: 'For my thoughts are not your thoughts, neither are your ways my ways saith the Lord. For as the heavens are higher than the earth so are my ways higher than your ways, and my thoughts than your thoughts.' Both the whole creation narrative as it is written down in Genesis 1 and 2, and the imaginative expression of it in Second Isaiah, leave the reader with a lively sense of what a later theologian was to call 'the infinite qualitative difference between God and man'. Theodore of Mopsuestia had summed up the situation in the words,

> It is well known that the one who is eternal, and the one whose existence came into being later, are separated from each other, and the gulf between them unbridgeable. . . . What possible resemblance and relation can exist between two beings so widely separated from each other?[1]

Given this difference between the natures it was inevitable that to secure the integrity of both they should each have an *hypostasis*. God and man in Jesus Christ each had his own nature and person; otherwise, they would be lacking in reality. Lan-

---

[1] Quoted by R. V. Sellers, *op. cit.*, p. 162.

guage was used which seemed to confirm the consequent dualism. Theodoret writes[1]: 'In Christ we contemplate the manhood through the sufferings, and we apprehend the Godhead through the miracles.' Scripture is examined carefully with a view to assigning different texts to different natures.

Probably the main psychological spring for the Antiochene attitude was a fear of confusing the two natures of Jesus Christ. Classically the name of Nestorius has been associated with carrying this fear to extremes and thus creating a dualism of the person of Jesus Christ. All the charges brought against the Antioch school may not be entirely justified. For example, it is difficult to see why H. R. Mackintosh[2] should say that they (Theodore and his group) could scarcely 'call Jesus more than a supremely inspired man', or that 'Jesus is man side by side with God'. Jesus is, for the Antioch school, and even for Nestorius, God-man. Whatever they say about 'the difference' it exists even for them within an ultimate unity. Nestorius says: 'Two perfect natures, both without confusion and without division, must be observed in our Lord Jesus Christ.' In other words, together with the 'no *physis anhypostatos*' principle, there is working the first constituent element in the two-nature model, drawn as we saw from the Bible itself, namely, the unity of the person of Jesus Christ. That it should be recognized by Nestorius who is classically associated with dualism, shows how necessary a part it is of the two-nature model.

In Eutycheanism

On the other hand, the traditional opponent of Nestorianism, namely Eutycheanism, takes the notion of the unity of Christ as the regulative element in the model, but it is nevertheless obliged to offer its account of how the two natures are to be reconciled with this unity. Eutyches is historically regarded as making two emphases, which gained him the reputation of heretic. First, he rejected the idea set forth in the *Formulary of Reunion* that Jesus Christ is 'out of two natures hypostatically united', and argued for the formulae: 'out of the two natures before the union' and 'not two natures but one after the union'.

[1] *Ep.* cli.
[2] *The Person of Jesus Christ*, T. & T. Clark (Edinburgh) 1912, p. 203.

It is nowhere explained clearly how Eutyches interpreted the transition from the two natures to one. He is not arguing for a transmutation of the human into the divine, nor does he countenance the swallowing up of the human by the divine. Secondly, he rejected the idea that Jesus Christ was *homoousios hēmin*. But he is, nevertheless, not a docetist in respect of the body of Christ: Christ had a *sōma anthropinon*, a human body. To his reply to his attackers, Eutyches lent a certain acidic quality by pointing out that there was no place in scripture where the phrase 'two natures' occurred, and whereas the term *homoousios* had no scriptural basis either, it did at least have patristic authority. Later the monophysites gave the ultimately logical grounds upon which a position like that of Eutyches might rest. Timothy of Alexandria, after enunciating the 'no *physis anhypostatos*' principle, affirmed that if there are two natures, then there are two *prosōpa*; 'and if there are two *prosōpa*, there are also two Christs'.

Comparing this conclusion which is the logical consequence of Eutychean thought with Nestorianism, we may note certain interesting points. First, both views combine an acknowledgment of the unity of the person of Jesus Christ with compulsion to express a judgment on how the two natures are related to this unity. Each throws the emphasis on a different point, but seeks to embody the other emphasis in some way or other. Secondly, both fail to establish their position by an outright and convincing appeal to scripture; at most in support of their own position, they are able to cite the absence of scriptural evidence for the opposite theory. Thirdly, most important of all is the way in which the 'no *physis anhypostatos*' principle yields such contrary interpretations of the person of Jesus Christ. At this early stage, we may begin to register a suspicion that the models in theology may not altogether merit the claim to the normative function which they so widely perform in this discipline. To give the suspicion a further degree of substance, it would be necessary to discover on what extraneous grounds (granted the absence of clear scriptural direction) one form of the model is to be (or was, by the formulators of orthodoxy) preferred to any one of the others. Meantime, we may proceed to another expression of the two-nature model.

The Chalcedonian definition

This time it is what is thought to be the classical expression of it that we shall consider, the Chalcedonian definition of the Faith.

> Therefore, following the holy fathers, we all unanimously teach that Jesus Christ is to be confessed to be one and the same Son, our Lord Jesus Christ, the same perfect in Godhead, the same perfect in manhood, and the same truly man, consisting of a rational soul and body, of one nature with the Father in respect of his Godhead, and of one nature with ourselves in respect of his manhood.... One and the same Christ, Son, Lord, Only-begotten, to be acknowledged in two natures (which exist in him) without confusion, without change, without division, without separation; the difference in nature being in no way removed as a result of the union, but rather the property of each nature being preserved and concurring in one person (*prosōpon*) and *hypostasis*.

It is now commonly acknowledged that this document is at its most explicit when it excludes the heresies. No Eutychean or Nestorian could find much comfort here. But when we try to advance beyond the negatives into a definition of the positive view which is offered there is not much to guide us, within the document itself. Clearly the unity which we took to be part of the two-nature is here affirmed. It is *one and the same* Son who is the subject of our confession and acknowledgment; no suggestion here of a Duad of Sons, or of two Christs. Even when it is said that there are two natures with two series of properties, nevertheless these properties concur in a single person and a single hypostasis. This fact can not be too often repeated, in reply to critics of Chalcedon who aver that it presents a dualistic view of Jesus Christ. In an almost literal sense, its first and its last words about Jesus Christ are that he is *one*.

As we have just seen, going on to look for the other features of the two-nature model, it is equally explicit that in Jesus Christ the two natures, human and divine, exist to their fulness. As eternal Son, he is consubstantial with the Father; here is the fulness of Godhead in no way diminished by reason of the incarnation. In his human nature, he is identical in essence with ourselves. The presence in him of deity in no way reduces his human nature to an illusion. It is possible in reference to Jesus to deploy two series of properties and to affirm them equally of the single person.

When we continue beyond that point and endeavour to identify the person to whom the two natures are attributed, it would almost certainly appear that it is the hypostasis of the divine nature of the Logos, who is the subject of the incarnational situation. I must say 'almost certainly' because however closely you look at the text it is difficult to see what the document really intends. This much is clear: there is no question of there being a second hypostasis or person. In other words, there cannot be a human hypostasis. This interpretation of the situation is at this point reinforced by reference to Cyril in whose writings it is somewhat clearer that the human nature of Jesus Christ is a *physis anhypostatos*. Whether Cyril tries to correct this patent violation of the principle of 'no *physis anhypostatos*' as H. R. Mackintosh suggests,[1] it has to be admitted that no attempt is made within the four corners of the Chalcedonian definition to make any such correction. It is for this reason that popular criticisms are levelled at the Chalcedonian definition: it offers an impersonal view of the human nature of Christ (anhypostasia). For us 'impersonal' means hard, callous, indifferent, even unloving; and it is a term with pejorative connotations, and in this context even damning implications. However, if we do apply it to Chalcedon—and there is no real evidence to suggest that we should—it is to be construed logically; or at most ontologically, as signifying that the human *physis* of Jesus Christ has no human *hypostasis*. It is assumed in the definition— a point that might be questioned—that this lack does not reduce the true humanity of Christ.

What must, I think, be said however is that so firmly is the 'no *physis anhypostatos*' principle rooted in the minds of all participants in the christological controversies of the fifth and sixth centuries that the vacuum which was created by the indecision of Chalcedon on the matter of an *hypostasis* for the human nature was one to be abhorred. It is a matter of consequent interest to discover how it was filled. Two possibilities existed and they were adopted. Curiously enough, they have both acquired importance for our modern handling of the two-nature model.

[1] *The Person of Jesus Christ*, p. 207.

94

Leontius of Byzantium

The first is traditionally associated with the name of Leontius of Byzantium (*c.* 485-543). That interpretation of the Chalcedonian definition which denied that the human *physis* of Jesus Christ had an *hypostasis* came to be known as *anhypostasia*; and it was in contradistinction to that view that Leontius sought to solve the same problem with his theory of *enhypostasia*. We have already seen how the 'no *physis anhypostatos*' principle had operated to give both Eutycheanism and Nestorianism; and how, also, the Chalcedonian position because of its failure to conform to the principle was in a rather unstable position. We have also seen how the original principle of 'no *physis anhypostatos*' derives very directly from the *Categories* of Aristotle, with a variation in specific nomenclature. Leontius, in giving the two-nature model his cash-values, draws more heavily upon the reserves of Aristotelian logic. He does so in two stages. First, to begin with, he elaborates considerably upon what is involved in the term 'nature' (*physis*)[1]. Following the Aristotelian conception of definition as *per genus et differentiam* he holds that *physis* is to be defined in terms of genus, species and essential qualities and properties. These terms all apply to what we would call the universal, i.e. 'nature' is that which the particular entity shares with all the fellow-members of the genus. *Hypostasis*, on the other hand, carries the reference to the principle of self-existence, particular and individual existence, of the sort the single entity has over against the logical group. The individual instance is distinguished from the other members of the group by peculiar characteristics of its own, *idiōmata aphoristika*, some of which are separable accidents (*symbebēkota chōrista*) and others are lasting (*symbebēkota achōrista*). So far nothing that makes any great difference to the basic interpretation of the two-nature model has been contributed by Leontius. Secondly, he affirms, in line with the Chalcedonian definition, that the human nature of Jesus Christ has no *hypostasis* of its own, but adds that it is not on that account *anhypostatos*. In fact, it is a *physis enhypostatos*, an enhypostatic nature; it finds its *hypostasis* in (*en*) the *hypostasis* of the Logos. Through the union with the divine nature, and as a result of not having an *hypostasis* of its own, the human nature

[1] See R. V. Sellers, *op. cit.*, p. 317.

is not absorbed. Its integrity is preserved through its sharing in the *hypostasis* of the Logos. The distinguishing characteristics of the particular man who Jesus was are then attributed to the divine *hypostasis* as well as the essential qualities of the species (man) to which he belongs. In this way he has secured a form of Chalcedonianism against the principle that it is impermissible, even impossible, to affirm a *physis* without an *hypostasis*.

This view was destined to have such a normative effect upon subsequent christology, both in the seventh century and in our own time, that it might be important to draw attention to three *prima facie* defects which it seems to have.

First, there is the criticism which Harnack made[1] so long ago, and it is echoed by H. R. Mackintosh,[2] that 'A pious Apollinarian monk would probably have been able to say with regard to the *hypostēnai en tō Logō*: "Apollinaris says pretty much the same thing only in somewhat more intelligible words." ' It is not unusual to substantiate this charge of Apollinarianism by pointing out, as does W. N. Pittenger[3], that on enhypostatic terms, the human nature of Christ has consequently no strictly personal centre; there is no ego around which the human life may move and upon which its experiences can 'home'. So the question has to be raised whether we may rightly ascribe to Jesus Christ the fulness of humanity, or whether in fact E. L. Mascall is correct in saying (though the very phrase is a self-condemnation) that Christ's human nature is an abstraction.[4] Clearly the enhypostatic theory is not Apollinarianism in the strict sense. For, while Leontius affirms that the Logos takes human nature, Apollinaris speaks more specifically of the *flesh*. There are sentences like: 'He who was once "without flesh" is now revealed "in flesh" as God incarnate (*Theos ensarkos*); but he remains still one and the same person'; and again, 'in Jesus Christ there is a unification of flesh with Godhead into one person'.[5] Leontius' position therefore only resembles that of Apollinaris in so far as both of them omit from Christ's person

---

[1] *History of Dogma* (ET), Williams and Norgate 1898, IV, pp. 233-4 n. 3.
[2] *Op. cit.*, p. 218.
[3] *The Word Incarnate*, Nisbet 1959, pp. 100-3.
[4] Quoted by Pittenger, *op. cit.*, p. 101.
[5] The quotations in this sentence appear in Sellers, *op. cit.*, respectively pp. 138 and 140.

the human ego. Even if we were to come at the question from the side of the trichotomic anthropology which Apollinaris employs, and to affirm that while Jesus Christ has a human body and mind, the human spirit is replaced by the Logos; we could find no clear parallel to anything in Leontius. It would perhaps also be a little premature to follow too closely Pittenger's interpretation of *hypostasis* as a centre of human experiences; for, as we shall see later, it is not immediately justifiable to translate what is a strictly logical concept into psychological terminology. What we could say, however, is that if the *hypostasis* is an essential part of what we associate with humanity (even if it is not strictly a part of human nature as *physis*), then in respect of his humanity, Christ is not completely one with us.

A second criticism, which might be raised against the *enhypostasia* of Leontius concerns the relation of the divine *hypostasis* to the human *physis*. In the Aristotelian paradigm of this relation, the *prōtē ousia* is the individual in which the *deutera ousia* is particularized, or at least it is the subject of the particularized form of the *deutera ousia* or the universal. In other words, the *prōtē ousia* is not just a blank area in which we stick the stamps of the *deutera ousia*; and we are at liberty to choose whichever stamps we wish for the purpose. On the contrary, it is so closely and integrally related to and congruous with the *deutera ousia* that it is understandable and describable only in terms of the latter. When we substitute for the *prōtē ousia–deutera ousia* relation that of *hypostasis-physis*, then we see just how difficult it is to remove the human *hypostasis* in the belief that the divine *hypostasis* can function in its place. The particularity and individuality of the man Jesus would be removed. In fact, it would be impossible to differentiate the *man* Jesus from the man Peter or the man John unless, in some way, the human *hypostasis* were retained.

A third criticism of *enhypostasia*, and one which could be the most serious of all, follows. If the *hypostasis* is understood to be so linked to the *physis* humanity that the latter cannot exist except as particularized in the several *hypostasis* then the redemption of the whole man is placed in jeopardy. For there is another important christological principle which we have not so far stated, which runs: 'What Christ did not take, he did not redeem.'[1] If, therefore, the *hypostasis* forms part of what it means to be human, then surely man's redemption requires that the *hypostasis* in a man be redeemed as well as his *physis*. It was this principle, too, which was the final basis for the rejection of Apollinarianism: because Christ did not take the spirit of man, but only his body and mind, the spirit of man was placed beyond the range of Christ's redemptive power. At this same point, any doctrine involving *anhypostasia* would be open to criticisms of being a defective basis for soteriology. In a very real sense any christology stands or falls by the soteriology which it makes possible, or implies.

Barth on enhypostasia

The enhypostatic christology has come to figure so centrally in Barthian theology that it may not be inappropriate to consider what Barth himself has said on the subject.[2] Drawing upon such writers as Hollaz, Polanus and Heidegger, Barth says that *hypostasis* meant the independent existence, the *propria subsistentia* of Christ's humanity. The human essence is adopted by the Logos and taken into unity with himself. Barth also feels that to say that it was a *homo*, a particular man, that was united with the Logos and not *humanitas* would allow a degree of autonomy to the human nature which would endanger the whole of christology. Barth does not explain the reason for his rejection of such autonomy, but one might guess either that it would imply Nestorianism, or that it would assign an unduly high place to the creature alongside the redeemer in the incarnation. Man would be a corredemptor. Barth is, however, aware of something rather like the difficulties we have been mentioning which the enhypostatic theory raises for the right presentation of the human nature of Jesus Christ.

He writes:

> The objection has often been raised that (the enhypostatic theory) seems to involve at an important point a denial of Christ's true humanity, a concealed or even blatant Docetism, since it must obviously belong to the true humanity of Christ that he should have an independent existence as a man like us.[3]

[1] Greg. Naz., *Ep.* ci.
[2] *Church Dogmatics* IV/2 (ET), T. & T. Clark (Edinburgh) 1958, pp. 49f.
[3] Barth, *op. cit.*, p. 49.

Barth seems to think that what the *anhypostasia*, presupposed in the enhypostatic doctrine, denies is the autonomous existence of the humanity of Christ. But it is more than doubtful not only whether the *propria subsistentia* is rightly translated as 'independent existence', and whether any christologian, even the most extreme Nestorians, ever thought of the human nature as autonomous. Accordingly Barth goes on in fact to mention what the anhypostatic theory would deny, namely, that the *humanum* exists in Jesus Christ in the form of an actual man. (One wonders if Barth would accept *prosōpon* as a fair translation of the term, and admit that there are then two *prosōpa* in Jesus Christ.) Barth makes a final break with the logic out of which the whole enhypostatic theory has been constructed when he says that Jesus Christ is a real man only as the Son of God: for it is no longer possible to see the original *prōte ousia–deutera ousia* distinction on which that theory rests in the relation of a 'real man' to the Son of God. Barth, I should say, is right in insisting upon the fact that in Jesus Christ the *humanum* exists in the form of an actual man (though how, having said so, he can still believe that in Jesus it was not a *homo*, i.e. a particular man, but *humanitas* that was united with the Logos, is difficult to understand). But if he still wishes to avoid both Nestorianism and docetism then he must revise his definition of the human *hypostasis* (as equivalent to 'independent existence') and of its relation to the human nature and to the divine *hypostasis*.

Ephraim of Antioch

It has always been of interest to me both that the quite radical difficulties which have been mentioned above in connection with the enhypostatic interpretation of the Chalcedonian definition have not inhibited the widespread development of this theory and that a possible modification of a theory which goes a long way to meeting some of the difficulties has not been presented in this setting. I am referring to Ephraim of Antioch, whose views have been preserved for us in the writings of Photius of Tyre, though I am concerned with one part only of his teaching and not with his ecclesiastical-political activities which were extremely varied. He maintains customary Chalcedonian positions, for example, that Jesus Christ is of one nature with the Father in respect of Godhead, and of one nature with men in respect of his humanity; that the two natures are not to be divided, for 'two natures does not mean two *hypostaseis*'. But what I would consider to be his originality emerges when he tries to explain the 'two natures in the union which is according to *hypostasis*'[1] by saying that while the two natures as such are not confused or compounded one with the other, the two *hypostaseis* are. Accordingly the *hypostasis* of Jesus Christ is a fusion of the human and the divine *hypostasis*: it is *synthetos hē hypostasis*. I am not interested to argue the authenticity of Photius' review of Ephraim's theories, or even the validity of Ephraim's other theological assertions. But it does seem that his theory of the *synthetos hē hypostasis*, the composite *hypostasis*, meets not a few of the difficulties created by the enhypostatic theory.

For example, first of all, by insisting upon the presence, in the composite *hypostasis*, of the human *hypostasis* it secures the wholeness of the humanity which Jesus Christ took, and firmly avoids the docetic and Apollinarian tendencies of the enhypostatic theory. Jesus Christ is a real man, not simply *humanitas* or the *humanum*, so really man, in fact, that it was possible for someone to write a purely human account of his life and death. In view of the different ways in which subsequent writers e.g. W. N. Pittenger, have come to use the two-nature model, this advance on *anhypostasia* and *enhypostasia* which doctrinally guarantees the integrity of the human nature of Jesus, is a genuine gain. On the strictly technical side it serves to protect Chalcedon from the common charge that it operates with an 'impersonal' view of the human nature of Jesus Christ.

Next, if we follow up the soteriological approach to Ephraim's theory, we could argue that it also secures the totality of the atonement of man. There is no hidden corner of his person, no aspect of his whole being which escapes the redemptive power of God. All has been taken, and all has been redeemed. Thirdly, it meets Barth's criticism that if we allow that the Logos took not only *humanitas* but also *homo*, then we affirm the autonomy and the independence of human nature. For, if the human nature has an *hypostasis* which is conjoined with that of the

---

[1] Quoted by R. V. Sellers, *op. cit.*, p. 323, *q.v.* for an interesting account of Ephraim.

divine nature, there is an end of independent existence and autonomy. God brings the human nature and its *hypostasis* under his control as its creator and redeemer.

Fourthly, Ephraim's theory has this additional advantage that it answers to the way in which we speak about the events of the incarnation. If we were to ask, 'Who is the subject of the stories which the Gospels record? Who took the loaves and the fishes and with them miraculously multiplied fed the multitude? Who suffered and died on Calvary? Who, indeed, was raised from the dead?', there could be but a single answer, 'Jesus Christ', and not 'the Son of God, *simpliciter*'. The latter phrase, 'the Son of God' would appear as the subject in a sentence answering the question, 'Who was incarnate?' Answer: 'The Eternal Son of God.' But after the incarnation, it is the God-man who is subject of what subsequently happens. In the end, this fact explains why it is so artificial, if not entirely erroneous, to try to assign some of the experiences to one nature, and some to the other. The God-man may 'have access' to certain experiences because he is divine, and to others because he is human; but ultimately it is he himself, and not either of his natures, who has the experiences and is the subject of them.

Difficulties for Chalcedonian christology: the doctrine of substance

I should like now to look at some of the difficulties which might arise for someone who today seeks to express his christology in terms resembling those of the Chalcedonian definition. Perhaps the first stumbling-block which he would encounter would be that of the doctrine of substance presupposed by all forms of the two-nature model, the ultimate distinction between a substratum or *hypostasis* and the nature (with all its attributes and accidents) which inheres in it. Locke's views on substance, springing from his rejection of 'depraved Aristotelianism', may first be stated in his own words:

> If anyone will examine himself concerning his notion of pure substance in general, he will find he has no other idea of it at all, but only a supposition of he knows not what support of such qualities which are capable of producing simple ideas in us.

This 'something I know not what' which Locke was prepared

to retain in its unknowable form because of the necessity to think of qualities as qualities of *something*, this self-existent substance Berkeley and Hume rejected, the first because he judged the very conception of substance to be self-contradictory, the latter because for him there was no empirical evidence for a substratum either physical or spiritual. The reinforcement of the older empiricism by modern forms of positivism has made it difficult for anyone to introduce into the modern theological scene thought structures which have such a decidedly Aristotelian substance-attribute character as the two-nature models. To have said so much might appear tantamount to having closed the case. Substantialism seems to be no longer a live option even for someone who still feels that there may be some defence left for metaphysics in general. Not quite, or, at least, not entirely.

It has always been a matter of great curiosity to me that ordinary people all of the time, and philosophers when they forget their calling and indeed their set attitudes, and are simply relaxing over a cup of coffee, should speak and act *as if* the substance-attribute distinction were an absolutely valid one. When the latter speak of the coffee being sweet and cold, and having rather unpleasant grounds swilling about in it; when they give a brief description of the characteristics of the new no. 6 iron which they have purchased; then they do not refer to constellations of sense-data held together by some form of inherent attraction, or of nuclear sense-data which are *maxima sensibilia* occurring at a certain point in space-time. They seem to be, by their speech, as committed to the basic Aristotelian language structure as the Philosopher himself. In other words, ordinary language with its distinction between subject and predicate seems almost to imply, if it is going to have any sense at all, something very like the distinction between substance and attribute, or rather substances and attributes.

I obviously do not wish to press this point too far. I am *not* saying that it was a good thing that subject-predicate analysis of the proposition should have exercised such a prolonged influence upon western logic; that it is possible to reduce all propositions to the subject-predicate form; or even that the subject of every sentence refers to a specifiable ontological existence.

Too much argument has flowed under logical bridges for one to be quite so naive as that. All that I do want to say is that there are many sentences—far, far more than the debunkers of the concept of substance realize—many sentences which are 'about' something or other, something which has qualities of a certain sort, behaves in a certain way, and is related to other existents in specific ways. This something or other is the subject of the sentence even if it is not its grammatical subject. The proposition thus asserted would be a non-sense if it were not about something other than itself, something which had qualities etc.

Words and things

William Kneale[1] summarizes one of the chief problems in Aristotelian interpretation when he asks concerning Aristotle's distinction between primary substance and secondary substance: 'Is Aristotle here classifying linguistic expressions or what they symbolize?' He gives as his own answer: 'Aristotle would certainly have answered that he was dealing with things and not with words. . . . He uses the differences between rules for different linguistic expressions as a clue to the differences between types of being.' It would seem to be possible, therefore, to take up a position midway between two extremes. Extreme one would be the view that Aristotle simply elevated a linguistic device into a rigid ontological structure, and that it is possible for us now to retain the linguistic analysis and reject the ontology altogether. In that case we should be trying to reduce ontological or metaphysical questions to purely linguistic questions. Extreme two would be to maintain an absolute correlation between the sentence structure and the structure of reality; and in that case we would be approaching very close to the idea that language presents pictorial representations of reality. As I have said we are endeavouring here to take up a mediating position —in line with what was said previously about the ontological status of models. The subject-predicate form, allied so closely as it is with the primary substance-secondary substance ontological distinction, while it may not stand in a relation of one-one correspondence to the latter, is nevertheless rightly understood as

[1] *Op. cit.*, p. 26.

one of the ways in which we may legitimately talk about reality. I would not press for all the detail of Aristotelian metaphysics, but unless our language is completely misleading we may fairly say that we expect reality to be not unlike how we describe it.

This short apologia for Aristotelianism is not as irrelevant as it may at first appear to be. For a very natural reaction both to the involvement of Chalcedonian christology with Aristotelianism, and to modern philosophical criticisms of the doctrine of substance may be to reject that christology completely. While it is of considerable interest that conservative theology should be both extremely critical of the Aristotelianism involved in Roman Catholic theory of the sacraments and so ready to embody something of the same metaphysic in its own christology; nevertheless it is worth remembering both that the argument from language may validate the doctrine of something very like substance and that the Chalcedonian christology is a much more live option than its origins would lead us to expect. I should like to sum up my position by saying that though in its original variant forms the two-nature model drew heavily upon the reserves of Aristotelian logic and metaphysics, we may still use it, without being so deeply committed in either of these directions. I cannot altogether agree with H. M. Relton[1] when he says that Leontius

> only employs the Aristotelian terminology as an aid to commend his idea, which in itself is quite distinct and independent of the philosophical setting in which its author places it.

I cannot agree with such an assessment of Leontius' theology, because in fact it is hard to see what 'his idea' would be without its philosophical Aristotelian setting. Nevertheless, what Relton says of Leontius albeit inaccurately, could be most truthfully applied to modern christologies, which continue to use the Aristotelian language without its full ontological implications.

The term nature: *a second difficulty for modern Chalcedonianism*

A second difficulty meets us when we contemplate the re-instatement of the two-nature model. It arises over the meaning of the term 'nature'. Let us look first at the human nature. The

---

[1] *A Study in Christology*, SPCK 1917, p. 76.

obvious starting-point is presented by the original form of the two-nature model. The human nature as such is what we would call the logical universal; and the definition of it would be *per genus et differentiam*, that is, by means of the genus to which the individual belongs and to the differentiating properties of the species. It is not an easy matter to define human nature exhaustively in this way; certainly I have never seen it defined with the precision shown by Plato in his definition of an angler[1] or by Susan Stebbing[2] in 'members of the university'. But clearly the kind of definition which is contemplated is in terms of man's belonging to, say, the genus creature, having differentiating properties such as rational, moral, religious, sociable and so on. It is inevitable that there should be a certain amount of reaction both against such a conception of humanity, as we shall see when discussing Jean-Paul Sartre, and against the idea that it was such a vague generalization that Jesus assumed at the incarnation.

I have already indicated that it is one of the defects of a strictly anhypostatic theory of Christ's human nature that it lands in that impasse. If we are going to avoid the impasse, the only solution is to revise the logic of universals at the basis of the two-nature model. Cook Wilson in discussing the nature of qualities once said that they are 'this-suches', being neither universals, suches (because they were *particular* occurrences of one kind or another, a particular blue, a particular good, etc.) nor absolute particulars, this-es, because they were instances of some *general* quality which other things also possessed; they participated in both forms of being; they were *this* and *such*, or this-suches. It seems surely that the same is true of the human nature of Jesus Christ. It is general human nature (the universal) which he shares with us, but it is also a particular of the universal, because he had all his own peculiar human characteristics. What we must not allow ourselves to forget is that it is the soteriological interest that is predominant in the discussion of the human nature of Christ—not the logical or even the metaphysical. It is important to acknowledge the universality of Christ's human nature, so that all men may share in the benefits of his atonement; but it is equally important to do justice to the

---

[1] *The Sophist.*   [2] *Introduction to Logic*, p. 436.

particularity of the human nature of Christ, in order to secure its reality.

J.-P. Sartre and human nature

Our discussion of the human nature of Christ would in a modern setting have a rather reactionary quality if we did not contemplate the strictures passed upon the very idea of human nature by Jean-Paul Sartre. While there would be very few English-speaking theologians who would follow the existentialism of Sartre, and he has had no one to play Bultmann to his Heidegger; nevertheless, I find his thought a rather searching catalyst for some of the dissatisfaction which many people feel when confronted with Chalcedonian formalities. For example,[1] take his affirmation that there is no such thing as human nature. Technically, the denial follows from his contention that when we are thinking of man, we must say that existence precedes essence, and from his denial of God's existence. Practically, this rejection of the very idea of human nature is his protest *against* the philosophical conception of man as the *res cogitans*, or of man as an instance of some universal man, the ethical, or the political man, *in favour of* man as he exists, who breaks into the world, who meets himself; man who protects himself towards the future, man who wills to act. It is an acknowledgment that man must accept responsibility for his own existence, both in himself and in conjunction with the whole of humanity. With such a protest before us, it would be difficult to revert to the rather lifeless and stylized conception of humanity offered in Aristotelian definitions. Besides, one would be rather insensitive not to observe that it is possible to state this protest as to the 'man' of religious thought, the man who provides evangelical fodder, the man at whom our sermons are beamed, the average member of the congregation, even the man who is the subject of salvation. Each one of these is a type, bloodless and universalized— indeed no man at all.

But perhaps the most interesting feature about Sartre's view of humanity is the way in which he succeeds in combining the individualism, which is a necessary corollary of a strong emphasis upon decision and choice, essentially very personal acts,

[1] I confine myself to *Existentialisme est un Humanisme*, Nagel (Paris) 1947.

and the universalism which saves his philosophy from being entirely subjectivist. In this respect Sartre would appear to correct what is a defect in Kierkegaard's theology, and one to which Kierkegaard was driven more than most Christian thinkers would be because of his violent criticisms of the Church of his time. Sartre, also in seeking a medium for the expression of the universal in humanity in the context of personal individuality, seems to be under a pressure similar to that which dictated the efforts of the exponents of the two-nature model who combined a theory of first substance with that of the second substance. Sartre uncovers the trans-personal or the universal element in the human situation in a number of ways. He says that when man chooses himself (affirms his existence, we might say) he chooses at the same time all men. When we act, we do so in the light of some universal image which we entertain of what man ought to be. Our value-structures, our range of responsibility includes the whole of humanity. Here is the lie direct to any criticism that existentialism is a form of moral, economic or political escapism.

Sartre imparts further depth to the dimension of universality in his doctrine of man by maintaining that the other is indispensable to my existence, and that the decision which man makes for himself is made within a world of other persons, with liberties set over against mine, which I must honour. Further, if it is not permissible to speak of a human nature which is a universal essence, it is possible to speak of the universality of the human condition. 'It is in no way fortuitous that modern writers should speak more readily of the condition of man than of his nature.'[1] 'His condition' is a phrase designed to cover the limitations under which man exists in any historical period, in any society, pagan, feudal or proletarian—to be in the world, to have to work, to be subject to death. In man's purposive behaviour, which can be understood by other men even though they belong to different epochs, Sartre finds yet another constituent of the universality of humanity. What Sartre has succeeded in doing for the modern understanding of the universalism which must be a part of our interpretation of human nature is that he has transferred it from the realm of logical universals

[1] Sartre, *op. cit.*, p. 68.

to that of human society, human beings in relation to one another, human beings in decision. There can be no going back from that secure position.

Finally, Sartre puts his finger upon that aspect of existentialism which has always made it attractive to Christian theologians, namely, his deep suspicion of ready-made moral codes to cover every situation in which a decision is called for. It is not that he is anxious to dispense with all accepted standards and to advocate immorality. What he does wish to emphasize is the necessity for human decisions in the face of human situations. In the face of such situations we have a sense of *délaissement* (abandonment). We do well to ponder the fact that such an experience may often be part of Christian existence. Christians are often called upon to act in situations in which there is no clear word from the Lord, and no clearly charted moral codes by which to pick their steps through economic or political obscurities. If the phrase 'being adult' has any significance—and I deplore some of its contemporary applications—it means at least this, that God asks us to make up our own minds, and not to be always hoping that we shall receive a coded programme from the moralists or a dictatorial fiat from himself. While therefore this discussion of Sartre's view is an intrusion upon our main theme, the justification for it lies in its indication of the task that confronts us when we endeavour to give modern cash value to the concept of human nature, one of the basic ingredients of the two-nature model.

Karl Barth and human nature

Having considered the terms in which Sartre deploys the notion of human nature, or more exactly, what it means to exist as a human being, we may with profit consider what a Christian theologian has to say on this same subject, namely, Karl Barth, when he deals with the doctrine of creation.[1] He develops his view of humanity in his commentary upon Gen. 1.26f.

> And God said, Let us make man in our image, after our likeness; and let them have dominion over the fish of the sea, and over the fowl of the air, and over the cattle, and over all the earth, and over every creeping thing that creepeth upon the earth. So

[1] *Church Dogmatics* III/1, Part 1, 1958, pp. 184f.

God created man in his own image, in the image of God created
he him; male and female created he them.

This commentary acquired importance in the study of the problem of women in the ministry in the Church of Scotland, in that
it was embodied, one must say, rather uncritically in the report
made by that Church's Panel on Doctrine to the General
Assembly in 1964. It came to have a quite unfortunate effect
upon the subsequent discussion by Presbyteries of that very
vexed topic. In brief, the case against women in the ministry
was as badly stated as that for women in the ministry. It is not
therefore altogether from academic reasons that one examines
the source from which the trouble came. The stages in Barth's
commentary are: first, he says that 'He created them male and
female' is an immediate interpretation of the previous sentence,
'God created man'. Secondly, the notion of 'the image of God',
the basis of man's creation, is not defined in terms of man's
peculiar intellectual talents and possibilities or of his reason, but
in terms rather of sexual differentiation. Thirdly, while admitting that sexual differentiation is 'common to man and beast',
Barth thinks that in the case of man 'the differentiation of sex
is the only differentiation'. Fourthly, the fact that man exists as
either man or woman is affirmed to be the paradigm of every-
thing that happens between God and man. Fifthly, the climac-
tic statement is that the fact that man is created and exists as
male and female will 'prove to be a copy and imitation of his
Creator as such'. (The addition to this anthropology made by
the Church of Scotland's Panel on Doctrine[1] reads as follows:
'The basic unit of humanity is not the individual human being,
male and female, but man-and-woman as one.' Matt. 19.5,
'They twain shall be one flesh' is quoted by the authors in support of this view, no reference being made, oddly enough, to
Gen. 2.24c, the original of Christ's quotation.)

It would obviously be unfair to burden Barth with responsibility for all the statements of the Panel upon man-and-woman,
but since their position is a logical sequitur of his theories, he
must accept his share of responsibility. These theories of Barth
cannot be accepted for the following reasons.

[1] *Reports to the General Assembly*, 1964, Blackwood and Constable (Edinburgh),
p. 761.

First, it seems to me that Barth's whole line of thought begins to go wrong at the very start, in his exegesis of Gen. 1.27. 'God created man in his image . . . male and female created he them.' Instead of absolutizing the sexual differentiation between man and woman, the author would seem to be doing precisely the reverse. He is saying surely that whether one is man or woman, one is still made in the image of God. In other words, sexual differentiation is irrelevant to man's or woman's being made in the image of God, or indeed of being an instance of the *humanum*. Surely among other things, this is one of the points that St Paul is making at Gal. 3.28: ' . . . there is neither male nor female: for ye are all one in Christ.' It is—I should have thought, clearly —here affirmed that once one has been baptized into Christ, and lives in him, then in this context sexual differentiation has become irrelevant. One could almost make a case for saying that sex, particularly with a capital 'S', the exciting kind you might say, is in the Bible associated with the sinful period between the fall and redemption. Pre-fall man is really, as we would tend to see him nowadays, rather sexless. It is not till after the fall that he is aware of being naked. After redemption, when the image of God is remade in him he appears once again to transcend sex.

Secondly, we are led, consequently, to think that by taking the Genesis story as the norm for understanding both the *humanum* and all man-woman relationships, Barth has allowed the marital relation to dominate his description. This defect is all the more destructive of the validity of what he asserts consequently, because the Adam-Eve relationship is not so much marital as crypto-marital; one dare not say pre-marital for fear of misunderstanding. Barth is led to the rather doctrinaire statements both that the sex-relationship is 'the original form of . . . all intercourse between man and man' and that sexual differentiation is the paradigm of all that takes place between man and God. Neither of these statements is true; and the fact that Barth's doctrines led to such improbable conclusions might have deterred him from affirming them.

Thirdly, Barth says several other unsatisfactory things on this same page.[1] For example, he fails to show clearly how sex differ-

[1] *Op. cit.*, p. 186.

entiation which man shares with beasts is nevertheless the basis of his differentiation from the beasts. Barth gives the curious reply that the only differentiation which man has is that of sex. It is difficult to resist the conclusion that Barth is here the victim of a simple logical muddle. He says in effect: 'Man (in general) = df. man/woman. Sex is the basis of differentiation of man from woman. Therefore, Sex is the basis of differentiation of man in general.' It is difficult to see how similar logic could not be applied to cattle, dogs, deer, etc., with the same non-compulsive conclusions. No attempt is made by Barth to show how the male-female relationship could possibly be a *copy* or an imitation of man's Creator. The main point which he is trying to make is that man is not man in isolation but in relation to his fellows: when he is I to a thou. In being so, he reflects the *societas* that exists in the Godhead, in the intra-trinitarian relationships of Father, Son and Holy Spirit. But this I-thou relationship could consist of man and man, or of man and woman, even when not married or in love with one another. There is no need to construe it in sexual-marital terms. In fact I doubt if such nonsense need detain us.

The really serious implication of this sexual definition of humanity is the christological one. If humanity exists only in the man-woman form, and if this form is interpreted normatively in terms of the marital relationship, then the humanity of Jesus Christ is incomplete, and the full demands of the Chalcedonian definition are not met: as touching his manhood, he will not be of one substance with men. It is no help to add, as some of Barth's apologists have attempted to do, that in the Church as his bride, our Lord fulfils this requirement. To advance this kind of defence is to do one or other of two equally unacceptable things. *Either*, it is to make the Church part of the human nature which Christ assumed at the incarnation and so part of the incarnation itself, and such a view goes far beyond even Roman Catholic theories about the Church as the extension of the incarnation. *Or*, it is to say that Christ at the incarnation did not have this female element in his human nature but acquired it when he created the Church. Such a view would be an admission that the humanity which Christ assumed at the incarnation was defective.

Human nature as the human situation

I wonder, therefore, whether if we were to try to deploy the content of the human nature of Jesus Christ, we would not, of all the devices laid before us, fall most readily into the kind of language which Sartre uses. When we speak of the Logos assuming human nature, we tend to deploy that phrase in this way. We speak of him entering into the human situation; taking to himself the sorrows, the broken relationships, the economic injustices, the political tragedies in which men find themselves; shouldering the burden of their sin, and taking from them the overpowering guilt of it all; and so making it his that he dies where they should have died the death that really was theirs. In taking human nature in this sense, he makes decisions; he senses the *délaissement* (abandonment), the utter loneliness of man forsaken by man, and the recovery assured to man who reaches that point of dereliction. In his own body, he has tracked the way back from that outer hell, so that men so placed shall for evermore know that one has stood there before them and now stands by them. To meet him at this point of total abandonment, to realize as St Anselm said *quantum sit ponderis peccati* is in that very moment to know the forgiveness that is offered them through Jesus Christ. In other words, what we should like to offer instead of a stylized definition of human nature is what I would call a situational deployment of that concept, which sets out what human nature means in terms of actions, decisions, conversations, addresses, parables acted and spoken, life and death, hell and resurrection. But at that point of deployment, we have, I feel, almost crossed a category barrier. At least, we are beginning to change models, to substitute for the two-nature model, the psychological model. To that we must now turn.

Before we do so, I want to make one concluding comment. It is that while we have been able to deploy one of the constituents of the two-nature model—the human nature—we seem to be rather at a loss to present a similar deployment of the other nature, the divine nature. We might cite briefly Tillich's 'ground of being' as a possible example of the reformulation of the divine nature; but we should be compelled to note that that reformulation is very much in the category of a stylized, logical form, or even formality. There is nothing quite comparable to Sartre's revision of what it means to be human, or even to Barth's. There may be, I believe, an explanation. It is that emphasis upon the doctrine of revelation has switched attention away from God to the revelation in which he is known. The revelation becomes all-important; and divine nature is deployed in terms of a 'life lived and a death died'. Because of this switch, we give notice that we intend to look also, therefore, at the model of revelation, for it is there that we should expect to learn of divine nature.

5

THE PSYCHOLOGICAL MODEL

SYNOPSIS

Whereas previously the history of textual, literary and historical criticism seemed to have invalidated the psychological model almost entirely, more recent considerations have called for its re-examination. Let us look first at the grounds for the old rejection of the psychological model:

1. The New Testament is a post-resurrection document; therefore it is impossible to reconstruct faithfully what was in Jesus' mind *before* Calvary.

2. The agnostic conception of the nature of historical knowledge which derives ultimately from Kierkegaard has influenced almost every major theological and biblical scholar of the present day; and has led to an almost universal denial of the possibility of all knowledge of the personality of Jesus.

The circumstances which are now leading to a reassessment of the psychological model are as follows:

1. Recognition of the true humanity of Jesus Christ entails some form of psychological interpretation of his life and actions.

2. Paradoxically, certain scholars (e.g. Bultmann, Bornkamm) who have been influenced generally by what I would call existentialist historical scepticism, nevertheless employ a form of the psychological model in their biblical exposition.

3. Expository preaching involves much psychological reconstruction of situations in which Jesus was involved.

4. The modern reinstatement of the doctrine of the *self* compels biblical and christological interpreters in the direction of psychological theory.

The psychological model has been employed by: (a) H. R. Mackintosh (in Kenoticism); (b) H. M. Relton (anhypostatic theory); (c) E. L. Mascall; (d) W. N. Pittinger; and in each case the possible heresy involved in the resultant christology raises the question of applicability of logico-theology to the psychological model.

The Psychological Model

WHEN WE turn from the two-nature model to what I have entitled the psychological model, it may at first appear that we
have moved away from the logically concise to something which
is definable only in the vaguest terms. But it must now be clear
in recollection that in fact the two-nature model is a deceptively
simple description which cloaks an amazing range of variation
from Nestorianism to *enhypostasia*. For this reason it should not
be unexpected if we encounter a variety of description under a
single title. Since the phrase 'the psychological model' is of my
own invention, it may prove helpful to indicate what it means.
The psychological model is a comprehensive description of those
interpretations of the person of Jesus Christ which both hold
that it is *possible* to speak significantly of the motivation, feelings, purposes, cognition and in fact the mind of Jesus Christ;
and go on to affirm that interpretation of this sort contributes
insights in christology which are obtainable in no other way
and for which there can be no substitutes. Discussions of the
psychological model have therefore taken two forms. On the
one hand, they have been concerned with the whole validity of
the claim to penetrate the *psyche* of Jesus Christ and to set down
in meaningful terms what the thoughts and purposes of a God-
man could possibly be. Sometimes the argument has never gone
beyond this point. On the other hand, when it has, the questions
have immediately arisen of how far one may go on this tack
and at what point a reverent agnosticism should begin to raise
its head.

Probably, however, no time could be less opportune than the
present for raising the matter of the psychological model. Günther Bornkamm[1] has written: 'The nature of the sources does
not permit us to paint a biographical picture of the life of Jesus
against the background of his people and age.' A few pages
earlier[2] he had asked the question: 'Shall we regress and once
again attempt a detailed description of the course of (Jesus')

---

[1] *Jesus of Nazareth* (ET), Hodder and Stoughton 1960, p. 52.   [2] *Op. cit.*, p. 24.

life biographically and psychologically?' His answer then had been: 'Certainly not. All such attempts are doomed to failure.' However, despite this shaky beginning, Bornkamm—to continue our original quotation—finally comes away strongly with the assertion: 'Nevertheless, what these sources do yield as regards the historical facts concerning the personality and career of Jesus is not negligible, and demands careful attention.' These quotations from Bornkamm state, then, the problem for the psychological model, namely, Has the recent history of textual, literary and historical criticism come to invalidate the psychological model altogether? We are obliged first of all, therefore, to look at that problem. But next Bornkamm does rather also suggest that whereas in the immediate past, the matter seemed almost to be closed at the point of agnosticism, now he wants to open a fresh door upon what he calls 'the personality and career of Jesus'. In other words, a change has come over the situation, and the psychological model requires a fresh examination.

Religious agnostic assessments of the psychological model

It is inevitable therefore that we shall start with those considerations which produced the agnostic assessment of the psychological model. These have become so much a part of the modern New Testament critical scene that it may be superfluous even to mention them. I only do so because of their relevance to the question of the psychological model.

The general assumption with which we may begin is that since the New Testament is the product of the primitive Church, it is a post-resurrection document. Sometimes the corollary is stated that the New Testament tells us more about the mind of the primitive Church than it does about that of Jesus. What it says of Jesus it says in the context of the knowledge that Jesus is risen and that his messiahship has been confirmed. There can be, therefore, it is implied, no possibility now of entering into the pre-Calvary situation, of penetrating to the uncertainty and the dubiety which may have been in Jesus' mind as the course of his life unfolded itself. The way in which this attitude is included as the unquestioned premise of what purports to be an argument can be easily illustrated from Bultmann.[1]

---

[1] *Theology of the New Testament* (ET), SCM Press, I, 1952, p. 26.

Some advance the following reasoning as an argument from history: The Church's belief in the messiahship of Jesus is comprehensible only if Jesus was conscious of being the Messiah and actually represents himself as such—at least to the 'disciples'. But is this argument valid? For it is just as possible that belief in the messiahship of Jesus arose with and out of belief in his resurrection. The scene of *Peter's Confession* (Mark 8.27-30) is no counter-evidence—on the contrary! For it is an Easter-story projected backwards into Jesus' lifetime, just like the story of the Transfiguration (Mark 9.2-8). The account of Jesus' baptism (Mark 1.9-11) is legend, certain though it is that the legend started from the historical fact of Jesus' baptism by John. It is told in the interest not of biography but of faith.

It is difficult to resist comment on this passage, because it illustrates so adequately the *inaequum certamen* upon which the psychological model is engaged. For example, in the first place Bultmann says that while an argument has been advanced to the effect that the messiahship of Jesus is comprehensible only if Jesus was conscious of being the Messiah, nevertheless 'it is just as possible' that belief in his messiahship had a quite different source, namely, belief in Jesus' resurrection. Bultmann does not really mean that the one argument is just as possible as the other. In fact, his whole ensuing discussion illustrates that since we are enclosed within the resurrection-faith, we are in no position to know anything of the messianic consciousness of Jesus. Any argument which involves knowledge of the pre-resurrection mind of Jesus is based upon a false premise. It is quite unfair therefore of Bultmann to introduce a theory which is in his judgment the only theory with the understatement that 'it is also possible'.

Secondly, the language of projection is introduced in this passage of Bultmann as a flat statement, whereas in fact it is both emotive and loaded. It is emotive because it entails an element of value-judgment, indeed, of rejection. It is loaded because it implies that whatever is projected is false. It is the language of psychological delusion, of inventions to atone for deficiencies, of phantasy to compensate for disappointments. The impression left by the passage from Bultmann is that the incident of *Peter's confession* is the attempt of the primitive Church to make a hero out of an ordinary drab mortal, to make a Christ out of a Jesus. It is certainly tantamount to a denial of any possibility of penetrating to the mind of Christ as it might have unfolded itself in his encounters with his disciples. The word 'projection' is almost like a signal to us to regard as inaccurate whatever follows.

Thirdly, it is rather interesting that Bultmann is not prepared to sever the link with history as we would ordinarily understand it. Of the account of Jesus' baptism by John, while using once again the language of rejection to dismiss it as legend (somehow 'legend' is a dead-for-ever word: it has no hope of survival after death as has the term 'myth' which goes through a series of metempsychoses), he nevertheless acknowledges that the legend did start from the historical fact of Jesus' baptism by John. The legend was not wholly up in the air: it was earthed in something that men saw and heard. In so far as the 'legend' might be quite permissibly understood to make known to us what was in the mind of Christ at the time of his baptism, the rejection of the legend is effectively the rejection of any psychological inroad into the christological situation. The historical fact of Jesus' baptism by John was, on this reading, an event with an outside but lacking entirely any inner structure of the kind assigned to it by the evangelist.

Fourthly, the keystone in the arch of Bultmann's pattern appears when he finally says that the purpose of telling the legend is to serve 'not biography but faith'. There are several unresolved problems here—for example, as to whether faith is aware that what purports to be something very like biography (in so far as it tells stories about parts of one man's life) is in fact a legend; or as to whether there is any appropriateness in the fact that faith should be supported by projections (on the face of it rather a major concession to the critics of Christianity). What is not made plain and what concerns us here particularly is whether faith is successful in penetrating within the psychology of Jesus; and if it does, whether it is competent to make statements about such psychology. There is, too, the unsolved problem of the validity of faith's statements about the mind of Jesus. Granted that they are not biographical, that is, not testable by the criteria of ordinary historiography; is it permissible to say that they would be admitted in a court in which special pleading may be made for statements asserted on the basis of faith? In this examination of a short extract from Bultmann, we have encountered many of the difficulties presented for the psychological model by the New Testament critical school which interprets the Gospel records as reconstructions of the life of Jesus from a post-resurrection stand-point.

Scepticism concerning historical knowledge

A second very important influence has led to widespread suspicion of the psychological method, namely, the sceptical or even agnostic conception of the nature of historical knowledge. I doubt if any single consideration has affected the whole of modern religious epistemology, as well as New Testament criticism and also understanding of the nature of faith, quite so much as the theory that all historical knowledge has a built-in probability coefficient. It is an almost unexamined premise of most modern theology which unites thinkers who, as we shall see, differ from one another in many other ways. My own opinion is that it represents the influence of Kierkegaard upon modern thought and it persists even when theologians consider that they have rid themselves of the existentialist elements of his theology and philosophy. On this ground, therefore, one of the most momentous assertions in modern theology must be Kierkegaard's statement[1] that 'Nothing is more readily evident than that the greatest attainable certainty with respect to anything historical is merely an *approximation*.' If we wish to give the obverse side of the coin which produces existentialism, we have to add the further quotations, 'There can in all eternity be no direct transition from the historical to the eternal, whether the historical is contemporary or not'[2]; and 'The transition by which it is proposed to base an eternal truth upon historical testimony is a leap.'[3] In view of the tremendous importance of these theories in subsequent theology and christology, we may in passing indicate that there are two possible sources for this assessment of historical knowledge as approximate, or, as we would say, probable knowledge.

[1] *Unscientific Postscript* (ET), Oxford University Press 1941, p. 25.
[2] *Ibid.*, p. 89.   [3] *Ibid.*, p. 86.

Sources of historical scepticism

The first source is strictly epistemological. If we divide all knowledge into truths of reason and truths of fact—as a long tradition in philosophy has done—then inevitably we shall tend to regard historical knowledge as concerned with the latter. If, further, we assign a coefficient of certainty to knowledge of truths of reason, then knowledge of truths of fact has tended to become a kind of second-class knowledge. This tendency has been arrested, admittedly, in our time with the new popularity of positivism, which is inclined to assign a, or even *the*, certainty coefficient to immediate sense-perception; though even positivism has felt obliged to retain the old gods of certainty in the new guise of tautologies. When we take the discussion one stage farther and recognize that Christian theology is inextricably allied to its historical foundation, then we are faced with the position that faith is bound to be a second-class form of knowledge, doomed to uncertainty about its subject, left with sneaking doubts in an area where above all one wishes for certainty, namely, concerning one's ultimate salvation. In this context, it is easy to sympathize with a theology which seeks to place a person's relation to his salvation beyond a peradventure, to give him some sort of assurance that there *is* a way in which he may reach his goal. That way is the leap, the leap of sheer decision. What has to be pointed out, however, is that the leap, the decision will remain utterly non-significant without some contextual historical knowledge, without some information about who Jesus Christ was, how he lived, what was the purpose of his death, what the nature of his resurrection. Even a leap cannot take place in a vacuum, nor can a decision be made except within a framework of reference.

But, secondly, a theological circumstance might be said to have led to the suspicion of historical knowledge in relation to faith. There is, I should say, a too great readiness, an almost indecent haste to be done with the detail of historical knowledge. There is not enough of a rearguard action calculated to save the historical foundations of the faith from the demolition of the sceptics. It is almost all too easy, and where things are as easy as that a theological reason is not difficult to find. Nor are we disappointed. There is behind this acceptance of the sceptical epistemology of history a fear that if historical knowledge were to turn out to be genuine knowledge, then faith would rest on something less than Christ himself. It would mean that a man might come to faith, not by means of a decision, but by a process of historical thinking. There is an ultimate difference between historical knowledge and faith; to move from the one to the other is to change categories. Once this separation has been made, once historical knowledge and faith are presented in the rigid terms of contradictories, no one who stands in that tradition will ever succeed in bringing them together again. Here lies the greatest single bedevilling feature of the whole controversy over kerygma and myth, a controversy which will go on endlessly unless we go behind it to the issue which Kierkegaard refused to face—how historical knowledge and faith are related to one another, for related they most certainly are.

Thirdly, it may be of interest to notice how widely this Kierkegaardian premise is accepted by thinkers who differ vastly in other ways. As long ago as 1929 Paul Tillich wrote these words[1]:

> The Christological question is the question of Christ as the center of our history. This question, moreover, is entirely independent of the problem of historical enquiry into the facts behind the rise of the Biblical picture of Christ. The exposition of these facts can only lend probabilities—and with respect to the historical Jesus, a very faint probability. No religious certainty, no religious belief can be supported by such researches.

I find Tillich here curiously ambivalent. Standing in the main stream of Kierkegaardian scepticism, he seems nevertheless determined to relate Christ to history, hoping to be saved from the uncertainties of history by means of the alchemy of faith. Tillich brings his analysis well within the range of logic and epistemology with his actual use of the term 'probability', which is a clear acknowledgment of the second-class character of historical knowledge, and of the necessity to remedy this deficiency by the introduction of some other source of knowledge.

[1] *An Interpretation of History* (ET), Scribner (New York) 1936, pp. 264-5. The original article appeared in *Religiöse Verwirklichung*, Furche-Verlag (Berlin) 1929.

There is, too, a passage in Barth, made famous by its quotation by D. M. Baillie[1] and latterly by Alan Richardson.[2]

> Jesus Christ, in fact, is also the Rabbi of Nazareth, historically so difficult to get information about, and when it is obtained, one who is so apt to impress us as a little commonplace alongside more than one other founder of a religion and even alongside many later representatives of His own religion.[3]

In this quotation, the scepticism concerning the historical figure takes an interestingly different form, namely, that of denigration of the person, or rather personality, of Jesus Christ; and it is worth asking whether this sort of judgment is not in fact equivalent to a rejection, albeit unconscious, of the scepticism of Kierkegaard. Brunner however provides the pure milk of the agnostic word when he writes[4]:

> Dependence on history as a science leads to a state of hopeless uncertainty.

Pure echoes of Kierkegaard come through in the next words.

> Therefore when a person refuses to build his relation to the eternal on anything so unsafe as historical science, he is acting rightly; for such a building is indeed a glaring example of building one's house upon sand.

We may round off this short review of the element of historical scepticism in modern christology with a further quotation from Bultmann[5]:

> ... the acknowledgment of Jesus as the one in whom God's word decisively encounters man ... is a pure act of faith independent of the answer to the historical question whether or not Jesus considered himself the Messiah. Only the historian can answer this question—as far as it can be answered at all—and faith, being personal decision, cannot be dependent upon a historian's labor.

Here the divorce between faith and history which has been en-

[1] *God was in Christ*, Faber and Faber 1948, p. 17.
[2] *History, Sacred and Profane*, SCM Press 1964, p. 134; which see also on pp. 125ff. for our present theme.
[3] From Karl Barth *The Doctrine of the Word of God* (ET), 1936, p. 188. Translation slightly amended by D. M. Baillie, *loc. cit.*
[4] *The Mediator* (ET), Lutterworth Press 1934, pp. 156 and 168.
[5] *Theology of the New Testament*, I, p. 26.

demic in this tradition from Kierkegaard onwards makes itself quite explicit without apology. This divorce has many wider implications for christology, which we might consider were we examining the historical model and its place in christology. For the moment we are interested chiefly in the implications for the psychological model.

Consequences of historical scepticism

Historical scepticism then has had observable consequences in the form of two denials, first, that it is quite impossible to construct a biography of Jesus; and secondly that later generations (that is, after the ascension of Jesus) have been cut off from all knowledge of the personality of Jesus. The first denial —namely of the possibility of a biography of Jesus—is obviously perfectly correct, if it means that we are unable to give, to use the words of Käsemann,[1] 'the fabric of a history in which cause and effect could be determined in detail'. The denial is correct, but one wonders whether the same kind of denial might not be made of any piece of biography, namely, that it is impossible to specify with any finality the ultimate springs of motivation that prescribe action. The danger is that we should become so bewitched by this denial that we fail to see that of itself it does not prohibit our making *some* valid historical judgments about the life of Jesus. In reaction against the defeatism and scepticism to which his above-quoted remark seemed to be leading him, Käsemann does admit very soon that 'there are still pieces of the Synoptic tradition which the historian has to acknowledge as authentic if he wishes to remain an historian at all'. Perhaps we ought to point the further moral, which Käsemann ignores, namely, that the authentic pieces of the Synoptic tradition ought to be accepted by the Christian theologian, if he is to remain Christian.

The second denial—that of contact with the *personality* of Christ—is one which to my mind is too readily dismissed as an irrefutable consequence of the previous denial. Once again it is valuable to notice what is being denied and what remains after the denial. What is being denied is that we know how Jesus developed psychologically from childhood to manhood; how he

[1] *Essays on New Testament Themes* (ET), SCM Press 1964, p. 45.

arrived at his messianic consciousness so-called; how indeed mind and will operated in his two-nature person. These are all significant and permissible denials. What is not necessarily implied by these denials is that we are ignorant therefore of what might be called 'the mind of Christ', of how he thought about the Father, about his own death, about men and women. It is not 'uncontrolled imagination' (Käsemann's phrase) that speaks of these subjects. Without some fill-in of that kind in our conception of Christ, without some understanding of what he thought or of his motivation, it is difficult indeed to say whom we are speaking about when we speak of Jesus Christ. He becomes simply an X recurring in a series of propositions about the kerygma; an X, moreover, concerning whose internal nature we are forbidden to speak even on the basis of the series of propositions. In short, my reply to such a view would be that if we are unable to speak of the *personality* of Jesus, we are *ex vi terminorum* forbidden to speak about Jesus.

This much is clear: if the psychological model is to be discarded, then modern christology is on the verge of reintroducing its own brand of docetism. The Word was made flesh, but made flesh in a manner which escapes all the ordinary psychological observations that one would make about a human personality. The early docetists wished to save the unchanging Logos the embarrassment of change and suffering, while their latter-day followers would save him the embarrassment of psychological qualities and characteristics; he is human but in no way known by us, which is to say in no way at all. The great tragedy is that at the very moment when psychological science has enabled us to understand more fully than ever before what is involved psychologically in being human, our scepticism should be preventing us both from understanding what form Christ's humanity took on the psychological side and consequently from knowing how much light the incarnation might throw upon the understanding of the human psyche.

The case for the psychological model: D. M. Baillie

But it would be quite wrong to give the impression that the case for the psychological model was one which had been lightly abandoned. In fact, circumstances both within christology and without have combined to secure for it a place or at least a live option on the christological scene. Let us look at them in that order, beginning with D. M. Baillie.[1] He puts his finger upon one of the most important circumstances within christology of significance for the retention of the psychological model: he drew attention to the more permanent contributions of 'liberal Protestantism' to the understanding of the person of Jesus Christ. These lay in the area of its definition of the humanity of Christ and they turn out on examination to lie in the psychological field. He mentions the human limits of the knowledge of Jesus Christ, the facts that Jesus grew in knowledge as he grew in stature, and that he is not to be considered to be absolutely omniscient from the moment of his appearance upon earth in the stable at Bethlehem. Sergius Bulgakov is reported[2] as having taken up this very emphasis in a Russian Orthodox interpretation of the person of Jesus Christ, holding that though Jesus himself claimed to be Son of God, 'even this apprehension of His own Personality remained subject to the conditions of human growth'. This emphasis represents a break with those elements in patristic and medieval thought which feared to compromise the omniscience of the divine nature of Christ by allowing any ignorance in his human nature. Baillie detects the humanizing tendency also in the preparedness of liberal theology to connect the miracles with Christ's humanity. Whereas traditionally they have been regarded as manifestations of the divine nature of Christ, liberal theology wishes to see them also as works of human faith. What he did, others could do: they too could 'move mountains'.

A further human circumstance to which Baillie draws attention is the character of our Lord's moral and religious life. His mission was fulfilled in terms of the human drama of faith fighting against tremendous odds and being victorious; his temptations had the quality of a genuine struggle against an evil power which threatened to overwhelm him; and the agony of Gethsemane and Calvary bore all the marks of human suffering, loneliness and rejection. Jesus too had a personal trust in God; he looked to the Father for strength and comfort; he, too, prayed, and looked for an answer to his prayer. So genuinely,

[1] *God was in Christ*, pp. 12ff. [2] *Op. cit.*, p. 13.

then, was the humanity of Christ presented by the school of liberal theology that there was no going back upon this insight. Perhaps this assertion might now have to be defended in face of the dehistoricizing tendencies of modern theological scepticism which we have just been examining. It could be defended, I believe, by reference to the way in which these same theological sceptics approach the New Testament literature: they do accept the human character of the Jesus of the records and ascribe to the primitive Church the deifying tendencies apparent in the Gospels. It is the latter which are particularly open to scepticism. The former are conceded as not in fact consolidating the claims of the theological picture of Jesus Christ.

Günther Bornkamm

D. M. Baillie was writing from the standpoint of the theologian. It is to me of greatest interest that Günther Bornkamm, with whose rejection of biographical and psychological description we began this discussion, should nevertheless embark, in the course of the book from which the quotations were taken,[1] upon a study which draws heavily upon what can only be called psychological material. He speaks of Jesus' sovereignty in dealing with situations in accordance with the sorts of people he encounters in them.[2] He has clear tactics for dealing with different people—drawing them out of themselves, meeting their objections, testing their sincerity and so on. His dealings with people as well as his public utterances bear the distinctive character of authority. He becomes genuinely involved in situations, angry at the power of disease, gently and tenderly blessing little children. And so the entire description unfolds itself, as Bornkamm rehearses the way in which Jesus understands and presents the theories of the kingdom of God, the will of God and the claims of discipleship; the narratives of his death; the messianic question and so on. This whole approach to the subject of Jesus of Nazareth, coming as it does on this side of the extensive scepticism which we have been examining, and seeming almost, to begin with, to be paying lip-service to it, would be quite impossible without some reinstatement of the psychological model, without some recognition that it is permissible to

---

[1] *Jesus of Nazareth.*   [2] p. 58.

discern what Jesus was intending, what his attitudes were in certain situations, how he understood his life and death and resurrection. Even if we feel that at times inverted commas ought to be inserted before and after the name of Jesus, this suspicion in no way alters the character of the exercise which Bornkamm is executing.

But before we hasten to say that Bornkamm is a rather odd exception, we ought to read again what Bultmann has to say on 'Jesus' Idea of God',[1] where he speaks quite freely of Jesus being certain that he is acquainted with the unswerving will of God; that he knows the world's futility and corruption in God's eyes; that he shares the Old Testament view of God; and in even more sophisticated terms, that he released the relation between God and man from its previous ties to history, and he desecularized man by placing him on the brink of eternity. Admittedly Bultmann, as distinct from Bornkamm, proceeds thereafter to the delineation of the primitive eschatological community's view of the message of Jesus, of God's judgment, the sacraments, the Holy Spirit, and so on. However, even when Bultmann comes to speak of St John's Gospel and its dominant ideas, he cannot escape speaking as if of Jesus, and not simply of St John's teaching about Jesus. Once again the psychological implications of the whole discussion come into evidence. The mind of Jesus or of 'Jesus' is still the subject of the exposition.

The conclusion seems therefore to be establishing itself that while there is widespread almost total rejection of the possibility of any psychological study of Jesus—a rejection shared equally by Barth and Bornkamm, Bultmann and Käsemann, to mention but a few—there is an equally inevitable tendency on the part of all of them to discuss attitudes, motives, ideas, reactions, and even feelings of Jesus. That rejection and this tendency are in the end of the day contradictory; and it can only have lasted either because the nature of the psychological model was misunderstood, that is, was taken to imply a total understanding of the psyche of Jesus, a rather preposterous notion anyway; or because more of these theologians were much less radical in their scepticism than their explicit statements would lead us to believe.

[1] *Theology of the New Testament*, I, pp. 22ff.

Expository preaching and the psychological model

Another circumstance within the theological field which has aided the revival of the psychological model has been the popularity of expository preaching. If one were to try to track down in human terms the secret of the power of the preaching of Professor James S. Stewart, he might at first mention the carefully chosen descriptive language, the constant practice of interpreting scripture by scripture. But the secret, I feel, lies in the way in which Professor Stewart so represents the biblical situations, so reconstructs the motives, attitudes, reactions of our Lord to those whom he confronts, that we ourselves are drawn into these self-same situations, ourselves confronted, challenged, judged, forgiven. Without some kind of psychological penetration into the mind of Christ, without some kind of exposure of his will, his purpose, his heart to the ears and minds of the congregation; not only would true preaching be nullified, but the way of our knowing Christ would be cut off.

At different times, and in different parts of the world, I have been required to give advice to divinity students obliged to preach before their training had been completed. In these situations I have said two things. First, that they take great care not to impose or inflict their newly learned theology upon the message of scripture which they were endeavouring to preach, that is, not to suspend theological essays on textual nails. Secondly, they should choose as the basis of their sermons situations from the New Testament or the Old which lend themselves to descriptive exposition and to interpretative development; that is, they should allow the message to grow out of the situation and out of its constituent parts. The purpose of such exposition is, stage by stage, on the human side to lead the congregation to the point of involvement and response to the present Christ. But that kind of preaching is destroyed by any scepticism we may have about the psychological model or the possibility of speaking validly about how Christ thought or about what he intended. The ever-continuing attraction of H. E. Fosdick's devotional literature, particularly of *The Three Meanings* may be traced to this source, that it takes as its overruling aim, the introduction of the reader to the person and personality of Jesus

Christ. Some of that literature inevitably bears the stamp of the theology of thirty years ago, though not nearly so much as the neo-orthodox critics of Fosdick like to think. But the aim no one dare gainsay, without indicating some better aim for devotional literature, and I know of none.

The contemporary interest in psychology: its relevance to christology

But if christology is going to react in any way to the culture within which it expresses itself, then it has to take account of certain circumstances in the contemporary scene which compel us towards a certain sensitivity to psychological questions. Anyone who has attempted to expound the two-nature theory to a group of senior Bible-class members will know that one of the very first questions raised in discussion afterwards is that of how a two-nature person operates psychologically. Leonard Hodgson[1] stated one aspect of the problem when he wrote:

> To-day it is the knowledge of the Incarnate Christ which is in the forefront of the (christological) discussion. . . . We ask now how we are to think of one person with two consciousnesses, with divine omniscience and human limitation of knowledge.

In other words, does the fact that Jesus had two natures imply that there were two streams of consciousness in his personality, two series of judgments, attitudes, reactions, each appropriate to the nature concerned? These questions arise even in the interpretation of biblical passages, for example, those dealing with Jesus' temptations, with his agony in Gethsemane, with his cry of dereliction from the cross. When Jesus prayed,[2] 'Abba, father, all things are possible unto thee: take away this cup from me: nevertheless not what I will, but what thou wilt', would it be correct to say that the human will was here aligning itself with the will of the Father, and/or with the will of the divine nature? A not uncommon reply to this kind of questioning is that it bespeaks an irreverently inquisitive mind, an indecently prying curiosity, which should be replaced by an adoring worship of the fact of the two-nature person. The fallacy of this reply is that it fails to appreciate how completely our generation has

---

[1] *And Was Made Man*, Longmans Green 1928, p. 10.
[2] Mark 14.36.

come to think in psychological terms, particularly and, I may add, appropriately, when it is thinking about *persons*. In what other terms can one, dare one think? This, it seems to me, is the point of bankruptcy for those christological theories which make such great play of rejecting the clues given in the New Testament to any understanding of the psychology of Jesus.

Christological doctrine is not alone in suffering from the contemporary organized suppression of psychology in the dogmatic reference. The doctrine of the Holy Spirit has been perhaps even more impoverished. Many accounts of the Holy Spirit and of his work stop short of the point where the issues for our day really occur—the point of his involvement in the decisions, the wills, the emotions, the cognitions, attitudes, character, reactions of ordinary men and women. We wrap up the whole situation in a parcel labelled 'paradox' and have nasty names like 'synergist' to fix on people who try to unwrap the parcel. This defect in our exposition of the work of the Holy Spirit has led to an almost complete lack of moral psychology in Protestant ethics. The relation of the human will to the Holy Spirit has been so enveloped in mystery that it has been left to extra-ecclesiastical groups like Alcoholics Anonymous to create a structure of moral recovery which has its ultimate foundations in the resources of the Christian faith. For this same reason, this silence concerning the relation of the Holy Spirit to the psyche of the human being, we have failed to provide our people with adequate doctrinal instruction because we do not possess the adequate psychological scaffolding with which to erect a devotional structure.

The doctrine of the self

A further circumstance external to technical christology but extremely pertinent to it which makes contempt for the psychological model somewhat old-fashioned is the quickened interest in philosophical circles in the *self*, the recognition of its status and importance. This interest and recognition have taken many forms. Perhaps the I-Thou philosophy of Martin Buber was the initiation of a process which spread into the whole of western Christian theology over the past thirty years, though there were more strictly philosophical intimations of this kind of interest before Buber. It was left to Buber to give it a language—I and Thou, as Austin Farrer once pointed out, are somehow different from you and me—and to indicate the lines which a personalist metaphysic could well follow.

A score of theologians took up the theme of the uniqueness and integrity of the self: Karl Heim in *God Transcendent*, Daniel Lamont in *Christ and the World of Thought*, Reinhold Niebuhr in *The Nature and Destiny of Man*, and perhaps most significantly for our purpose, John Macmurray in *The Self as Agent*, to mention but a few; and it was embodied in the whole existentialist movement. The self is not a loosely connected series of phenomenal occurrences; it is not a complex of mental states and processes in balanced co-ordination; it is a centre, a standpoint, an agent to make decisions and to fulfil itself in action rather than in knowing, a subject in its own right to be treated and dealt with in a manner appropriate to itself. Because of the ultimate destiny under which Jesus lived, preached and died; because of the profound character of the decisions which he had to make; because of the manner in which he related himself to the totality of existence, to God, to human guilt, to death; his selfhood has come to have a peculiar fascination for a generation which in its thinking about the human situation operates naturally and freely with dramatic psychological models of the self. It would be absurd to ask a generation which thought in such terms suddenly to discard the central idiom of its thought in its understanding of Jesus Christ. It is just this absurdity that is proposed by those who insist that the psychological model be rejected, and that we speak no longer in terms of the personality, that is of the self, of Jesus. In that rejection, it should be noted, we abandon also the insight which knowledge of him can throw upon human selfhood.

These, then, are some of the circumstances which make a wholesale abandonment of the psychological model a hazardous adventure. They have also induced certain christological writers to offer forms of the psychological model as a basis for christology. To these we shall now turn.

Kenoticism related to the psychological model

The psychological model played a great part in one particular christology which exerted a dominant influence in Britain for some fifty years of the present century, namely the Kenoticist christology. This influence operated in Britain through the writings of P. T. Forsyth and of H. R. Mackintosh. However critical we may be of Kenoticism, and it has become fashionable nowadays to reject this theory, it is important to realize what the problem was which Kenoticism was trying to solve. It was an attempt to meet two demands: the first, the orthodox christological affirmation of the two natures of Jesus Christ, and the other the necessity to acknowledge the full humanity of Jesus Christ in the terms established by liberal theology. The latter demand was not an unduly difficult one to meet. The human nature of Christ was presented very much as humanistic or liberal interpretations had pictured it: the apologetic value of Kenoticism lay in its adopting as much of that sort of interpretation as possible. Kenoticists varied however when they came to define how exactly the divine nature was to be constituted. The spectrum of variation has ranged from the assertion that the divine nature is represented by the divine *hypostasis*, through such as that the Logos 'reduced himself to the Jesus of a human soul' (Gess) or that he surrendered 'the glory and the prerogatives of deity' (H. R. Mackintosh) to the quite positive statement of Thomasius of Erlangen that while the Son of God laid aside his omnipotence, omnipresence and omniscience, he nevertheless retained in the incarnate life his love, holiness and justice. But the claim held in common by all the exponents of Kenoticism is that it is the Logos, however fully or indifferently characterized, who is the subject of the human life, activities and experiences.

For a number of years now Kenoticism has been criticized severely—by William Temple and earlier by Dorner, and in more recent times by D. M. Baillie and W. N. Pittenger—on what have now become traditional grounds. First, Kenoticism introduces what can only be regarded as a rather improbable transaction within the Godhead prior to the incarnation, according to which Jesus arranges to come to earth with some only of his divine attributes. Secondly, if this demission of power, this depotentiation, is genuine then other quite fundamental problems arise over how and by whom the cosmic functions previously fulfilled by the Logos are now being executed. Thirdly, there is genuine doubt over the ontological continuity between the Logos and Jesus. So great is this doubt that the question must be asked whether Kenoticism does not effectively violate the Chalcedonian thesis of the perfect Godhead of Jesus Christ. The divine nature is so reduced as to be no longer identifiable as such in its completeness. Fourthly, since the *kenosis* is associated with the incarnation, and since with his glorification at the ascension the Logos resumes his full stature of deity in a *plerosis*; it is no longer possible to affirm that in glory the Logos retains his human nature.

All that has been noted in the now traditional criticism of Kenoticism can be made without much modification to the views of H. R. Mackintosh stated in his *The Person of Jesus Christ*. His compromising of the divine nature of Jesus Christ is clearly illustrated by such sentences as the following[1]:

> (Jesus') life on earth was unequivocally human. Jesus was a man, a self-consciousness; of limited power, which could be, and was, thwarted by persistent unbelief; of limited knowledge . . . ; of a moral nature, susceptible of growth and exposed to lifelong temptation, of a piety and personal religion characterized at each point by dependence upon God. In short, He moved always within the lines of an experience humanly normal in constitution, even if abnormal in its sinless quality.

So much is standard issue for Kenoticism. The remarkable part of Mackintosh's theory—a part which has thrown more light upon more christological theory than the whole of his Kenoticism—appears when he rounds off his Kenoticism with a statement about revelation, namely 'The Eternal has revealed himself notably in a human being who lived at the beginning of the Christian era.'[2] He had anticipated this view four pages earlier when he spoke of 'the fact of Christ' becoming 'for us a transparent medium through which the saving grace of God is shining'. Mackintosh's christological progression has therefore been somewhat as follows. He began with an allegiance to the Chalcedonian type of two-nature theory, which he modified in two directions, first, by reducing very considerably the content

---

[1] *Op. cit.*, pp. 469f. [2] *Op. cit.*, p. 471.

of the divine nature, and by affirming the totally unequivocal character of the human nature (ignorant, weak, etc.). So impressed is he now by the humanity of the human nature of Jesus that he seems to be aware that it would be compromised if it existed in one person with the divine nature. This problem he solves by saying that the human nature *reveals* the divine nature which does not therefore exist *in* Jesus Christ in the same way as does the human. There is, I feel, a certain prophetic quality in this part of Mackintosh's thought in so far as it anticipates both the role that the concept of revelation is going to play in christological theory in the fifty years following his writing and the difficulties created by the introduction of the model of revelation into the christological scene. That is the subject of our next discussion.

Modern enhypostatic theory modified in terms of the psychological model

In the meantime, I should like to examine another form of the psychological model, namely, that attempted by H. M. Relton in *A Study in Christology*.[1] Relton adopted as the basis of his christology the enhypostatic theory in the form propounded by Leontius of Byzantium, the theory that while there are two natures in Jesus Christ, only one, the divine nature, has an *hypostasis*. The human nature is not allowed to be *anhypostatos*, but is enhypostasized in the divine *hypostasis*. When this theory is looked at from a psychological point of view, then the question inevitably arises of whether in Jesus there are therefore two streams of consciousness. Relton attacks this problem quite boldly, almost foolhardily, by saying at once that there is in Jesus Christ one single consciousness and not a double self. The single consciousness is that of the God-man. Before he was incarnate, the divine Logos was already possessed of whatsoever he required to be able to lead a truly human life. In other words his deity was not a disqualification for his being human, something of which he had to be shorn to enable him to live a genuinely human existence. For a further amplification of his position he chooses a view once stated by Apollinaris, that there is in God a human element. In other words, 'human' and 'divine' are not two contradictory terms: they are complemen-

1 SPCK 1927.

tary, 'the less being included in the greater'. Divinity is perfect manhood. The God-man may be said therefore to live a truly human life because he was always the Son of God and always had within his divine nature the perfection of humanity. Indeed manhood is at its highest and best when united with God. There is no difficulty for Relton in affirming that the Logos is the *hypostasis* of the human nature of Christ, as of the divine, and that his consciousness is unitary, and develops according to the laws of growth governing finite human consciousness.

It is important to notice at the start of any discussion of Relton's view what exactly he has done. He has translated the term 'nature' by the term 'consciousness', and he is even prepared to say[1] that the unity of Christ is to be located in the unity of his self-consciousness. He rather blunts the edge of the equation, however, by going on to say that the self-consciousness of the God-man is the subject of the two natures. Quite apart from the question of whether it is permissible to equate 'nature' and 'consciousness'—a confusion of categories which we shall later examine—it makes a nonsense of the whole exercise if we subsequently try to combine them in the same sentence, using them as if they still had different meanings.

Secondly, Relton is certainly making a sound point when he says, by implication, that traditionally in christology too much has been made of the contradiction between human nature and divine nature, and that more should be done to explore the appropriateness of human nature to the purposes which God is seeking to achieve in the incarnation. At the same time, however, the statement that there is an element of the human in God is much too vague to be of any great help. For we require to know what features of humanity are in God, say, will, intelligence, or what? Without some indication of that sort, the statement is simply the converse of saying that man is made in the image of God—the converse, or more naively, a logical implication, for if man is made in the image of God, by definition there is in God an element of the human.

Further, thirdly, no good purpose is served by saying that divinity is perfect humanity. For quite apart from the fact that this view begs the question of whether there is more to divinity

---

[1] *Op. cit.*, p. 226.

than the perfection of humanity, it leads to unsatisfactory conclusions in three ways. By his emphasis upon the identity of human nature and divine nature, Relton removes all necessity for the incarnation. God, on these terms, already has human nature: he does not require to 'assume' anything. On the other hand, if Relton really does mean that there is a difference between ordinary human consciousness and divine consciousness, then he is guilty of heterodoxy in either of two ways. Either, he may be saying that whereas ordinary men have ordinary consciousness, in Jesus Christ this form of it is replaced by the divine form, i.e. perfection. This view is effectively Apollinarian. Or, he may simply be saying that the human nature is absorbed in the divine consciousness, and we have then one nature, one consciousness—which is Eutycheanism. In a word, the composition which Relton prepares consists of too many constituent parts; it follows too closely the directions to the bride to get 'something old, something new, something borrowed . . . ', to achieve any really stable conclusions.

E. L. Mascall and the psychological model

A further example of the way in which the psychological model might be made to work comes from the writing of E. L. Mascall,[1] even although he is himself rather hesitant about discussing the psychological implications of the enhypostatic two-nature theory which he accepts. Starting from the now famous remark of Leonard Hodgson's that the question of the knowledge of the incarnate Lord is the major christological issue of recent times, and admitting, rather reluctantly one feels, that 'the question of Christ's human consciousness having been raised we cannot avoid discussing it',[2] Dr Mascall propounds his own theory of the nature of the knowledge which Christ had. It has wrongly been assumed in the past that there are only two alternatives on this subject. The one is that of Chalcedonian and patristic christology according to which the knowledge of Christ is co-extensive with the knowledge of the Logos, and the babe in the manger is thought to be contemplating the procession of the Holy Ghost, the theorems of thermodynamics, the novels of

[1] *Christ, the Christian and the Church*, Longmans Green 1946, pp. 53ff.
[2] *Op. cit.*, p. 54.

Jane Austen and the date of the battle of Hastings. The other is the kenoticist reaction to that sort of christology, and its view is that Jesus Christ being truly human shares in human ignorance, as we have already seen H. R. Mackintosh believed. Jesus Christ in his earthly life acquired knowledge in the same way as does every human being, by sensation and perception, by trial and error, by being taught and by learning.

There is a third possibility, namely, that there should be two kinds of knowledge in the human mind of Jesus: first, that which he has acquired in a purely human way as we have just described it and secondly that which has been infused into it from the omniscient divine mind. There is the necessary human limit to the extent of this infused knowledge so that the possibility never arises of the two bodies of knowledge becoming identical with one another. The other circumstance which is relevant to the communication of knowledge from the divine mind to the human is the precise requirements of the situation in which Jesus is placed. In other words, we are asked by Dr Mascall to conceive of a 'stratification' of knowledge in Jesus' human mind, and we are offered, comparing natural things with supernatural, an example. A 'perfect' lecturer, knowing thoroughly both his subject and the capacities of his class will impart to them at each stage of the course just as much knowledge as they can competently absorb. Even where he is himself aware of short-cuts he will take a long way round, because he knows that the class will be able to follow the latter. The illustration is defective, of course, in that the lecturer's own knowledge has in its turn been acquired, whereas the divine nature of Jesus Christ possesses full knowledge from all eternity.

Dr Mascall was extremely reluctant in the first instance to submit this psychological model, and it is therefore perhaps more than a little unfair to press him concerning it. Yet it seems to me that there are two difficulties which his exposition must eventually encounter. On the one hand, if it is assumed that the divine person is the subject of the knowledge of both the divine mind and the human mind, it is difficult to avoid the conclusion that he both knows and does not know the same fact at the same time. There is no escape from this difficulty by saying that this knowing and not knowing a certain fact is a common feature of normal psychology. For example, a certain piece of information which I once knew may not be in the process of actually being recalled by me at a given moment, and I may in one sense be truthfully said not to know it at that moment. As soon as it is recalled for me by someone else, I may again quite truthfully say that, of course, I knew it. I both did not know and did know this piece of information. That example cannot be validly extended to the knowledge of Jesus Christ. For if the divine person knows some fact through the omniscience of the divine nature, this fact does not require to be recalled for him by someone else in order that he should know it; and the ignorance of the human nature is the ignorance of never having known, and not the ignorance of the mind which once knew and is not in process of actively recalling a given fact. Therefore, if the divine person is taken as the subject of the two natures, he is both omniscient and ignorant at the same time.

On the other hand, I do feel that the example of the 'perfect' lecturer mentioned by Dr Mascall points to a rather different construction, namely, that the two natures are really rather like two persons, one communicating information to the other as need requires, and as capacity allows. This construction avoids the difficulty of the previous interpretation of Mascall's view, and it does entail a genuine ignorance on the part of the human nature, and genuine knowledge on the part of the divine nature, there being no *tertium quid* omniscient and ignorant at the same time. But the price at which this rationalization of Dr Mascall's view has been achieved is one which is higher than he would be prepared to pay—the price of heresy, in fact, the Nestorian heresy; for the two natures have been converted into two persons. But the illustration, based as it is on two persons, a lecturer and his class, does at least point in the Nestorian direction.

W. N. Pittenger

The mention of Nestorianism leads us naturally to one who is not afraid of the label, Professor W. N. Pittenger.[1] He is very sensitive to the claims of enhypostatic christology but, criticizing it for the *anhypostasia* which it presupposes, he affirms that it fails to do justice to the full humanity of Christ. The human nature

[1] *The Word Incarnate*, Nisbet 1959.

of Jesus, on these terms, lacks any truly human centre. The situation is not saved if we affirm that the divine *hypostasis* is the personal centre of the human nature: in fact, the lack of a human centre is thereby acknowledged. Previously[1] we drew attention to the implicit Apollinarianism in enhypostatic christologies; but Dr Pittenger prefers to charge it with Eutycheanism —if the humanity of Jesus Christ has no human creaturely centre, it is eventually subsumed into and lost in his divinity— and to point out its total failure to do justice to the Gospel portrait of the Man among men, who prayed to the Father, who declared himself ignorant of the Father's will and who was broken in weakness in the face of death. Dr Pittenger summarizes his own position thus[2]:

> The Eternal Son or Word so appropriated and employed the humanity which by divine providential operation was conceived and born of Mary that he possessed in that humanity an organ for self-expression which was adequate to his purposes, while the human life which was conceived and born of Mary so appropriated and expressed the Eternal Son or Word that such an organ was in fact available for the Son's or Word's purposes among men.

In his criticisms of E. L. Mascall and in his support for the Antiochene school, he shows how far he is prepared to go in assigning to the human nature of Jesus Christ a human centre, and to accept the possibility of the Nestorianism of two persons in Jesus Christ. The impression is confirmed when[3] he finds the most integrated and complete union of Godhead and manhood is one in which God graciously indwells in man and man responds fully and freely to God in love, a union in which God reaches farthest into man's life and man responds most richly to God.

Here we have the most explicit affirmation of the psychological model. In fact, this model becomes normative for Dr Pittenger of all the well known christological formulae—from the simple Gospel statements about a man Jesus to the sophistications of enhypostatic theory and Barthian theology. I should like to take up one or two points in the views above summarized: First of all, while it is only right to do full justice to the humanity

---

[1] See above, p. 96.   [2] *Op. cit.*, p. 92.   [3] *Op. cit.*, p. 188.

of Jesus Christ by assigning to it a human centre, and Dr Pittenger's criticisms of *enhypostasia* are entirely valid, one wonders whether he really faces the difficulties of Nestorianism. These difficulties are in fact more serious for him than they were for classical Nestorianism, for while the latter might be able to say that it was dealing with a metaphysical structure and was not in any way obliged to show 'how it worked' Nestorianism based on the psychological inadequacies of its rival theories cannot afford to ignore such difficulties. There is the problem, raised by Dr Hodgson and Dr Mascall, of the nature of the knowledge of the incarnate Lord. This is not a problem if the two natures exist in two entirely separate persons; but when these two persons are one being, we have the old problem of Jesus Christ being omniscient and ignorant at the same time, as well as being omnipotent and weak, omnipresent and located in time and space.

Secondly, in taking the compresence of God and man in a man striving perfectly to respond to the grace of an indwelling God, as the analogue of the presence of two natures in Jesus Christ, Dr Pittenger fails to see that christology has always assumed as a first premise that God is not in Christ in the same way as he is in ordinary men or even in saints; and that this difference has been *the* christological problem. We do not solve that problem by ignoring it or denying it. Thirdly, Dr Pittenger's own account of the relation of the two natures to one another in Jesus Christ would appear on closer examination to be rather complex. He makes two points. On the one hand the human life conceived and born of Mary so appropriated to himself the Eternal Son (Word) and expressed that Word (stage one) that he was available for employment by that Son (Word) for the execution of his purposes (stage two). On the other hand, the Eternal Son (Word) so appropriated to himself the human life conceived and born of Mary, and employed him (stage one) that he became an organ for his self-expression (stage two). In these two sentences the order of certain events—the appropriation of Eternal Son by human life and of human life by Eternal Son, the expression by the human life of the Word, the execution by the human life of the purposes of the Son, the employment of the human life by the Son—is so variously stated as to leave us in doubt whether Dr Pittenger is prepared or not to run the gauntlet of the criticism of Adoptionism. Certainly the Nestorianism is here explicit.

Conclusions concerning the psychological model

I should like to summarize now some of the conclusions which are beginning to emerge from this investigation of the psychological model. The first, and perhaps the most obvious by now, is that when the psychological model is made the basis of christological expansion it apparently invariably ends in some form of heresy—heresy judged, that is, by the Chalcedonian definition. In the older conservative theology the heresy was that of docetism: no genuine reality or growth was allowed to the human nature of Jesus Christ. In the enhypostatic modifications of the Chalcedonian christology, an Apollinarianism always suspected of being present in the purely dogmatic presentation clearly comes into view. In Relton, in spite of his enhypostatic sympathies, it is Eutycheanism which characterizes his christology. Pittenger is committed to Nestorianism, because he feels that on no other terms can we be sure of safeguarding the genuine and complete humanity of Jesus Christ. Even Mascall whose dogmatic sensitivity must be well nigh impeccable employs illustrations which make sense only in Nestorian terms. In short, there is scarcely a single classical christological heresy which has not been reproduced in the modern period in the effort to produce a working psychological model for christology.

Secondly, so comprehensive is the evidence that it is difficult to avoid the view that the fault does not lie simply in the inability of the searchers to find the successful orthodox psychological model. There would almost appear to be something inherently logically impossible in the whole enterprise. Perhaps we ought to qualify that conclusion by adding—so long as we accept the Chalcedonian two-nature model as the norm for the expansion of the psychological. There's the rub. Some years ago now Dr Mascall made illuminating comments on this very conclusion, though it is a pity that he did not pursue its proper implications. He said,[1]

Christological doctrine is not primarily psychological but onto-

---

[1] *Christ, the Christian and the Church*, p. 54.

logical. No amount of discussion of our Lord's psychology can have any *direct* bearing on the Catholic creeds and the Chalcedonian definition.

While these comments, as I say, are illuminating for our present discussion, they are not altogether accurate. Dr Mascall seems to have forgotten the extent to which psychological considerations were very much part of the decades of christological controversy which finally yielded the Chalcedonian definition. The Arians—whatever we say about them—like most heretics (and indeed, if the scriptures be accepted literally, also the Devil himself) all knew their scriptures very well; and they argued from a lively knowledge of what Jesus said and did, of how he felt and suffered and from many psychological considerations. It is quite wrong to present the Chalcedonian definition as if it were the outcome of a series of meetings of the middle-eastern section of the Aristotelian Society. Nor is it easy to persuade any thinkers bred in schools of pragmatism to admit Mascall's implied distinction between logic and psychology. Nevertheless, with these reservations I am convinced that his judgment is a sound one—though I think that it ought to be stated the other way round, to meet my first objection, thus: the Chalcedonian definition can have no *direct* bearing upon the discussion of our Lord's psychology. If that judgment is accepted, then we have put to an end the necessity to judge and dismiss every psychological model because it has failed the Chalcedonian test. The movement from the two-nature model to the psychological model, the application of the norm of the one to the other is a category error.

Thirdly, if we pursue the implications of that position, then we shall give up trying to translate the ontological categories of the two-nature model into psychological terms, and saying that $a = b$ and $c = d$ and so on. There is no such dictionary. Even words like nature or person which might occur in both contexts are not equivalents. It was at such a point that the expansion of the psychological model by writers such as Relton and even Mascall failed: they felt obliged to remain within distance of the two-nature model and to be plotting their position by reference to it. The future of the psychological model, therefore, lies not in its validation by a Chalcedonian test, but in the explanation and expansion of all its own possibilities. To quote Professor G. S. Hendry,[1] who was examining this very subject though for a rather different purpose:

> If Christ is true and complete man, it must be possible to raise the question of his person in terms of psychology and ethics . . . for it is of the essence of manhood that it is susceptible to ethical and psychological interpretation.

That process of ethical and psychological interpretation remains as necessary a part of christological thought as do the ontological and existentialist analyses which seem today to dominate the scene.

Finally, we have already noticed[2] that H. R. Mackintosh moved from a kenotic form of the psychological model to what we shall later be calling the revelation model. Before we leave the psychological model we may note how appropriate that transition is. The psychological model understandably dealt more with the human nature than the divine. Professor Hendry's point was that it is of the essence of *manhood* to be susceptible to psychological interpretation. If the implied restriction is imposed and the divine nature seems automatically to elude the psychological model, some mechanism becomes immediately necessary to relate the human nature to the divine. It enables us to probe the human nature to its deepest limits, while exempting the divine nature from that sort of analysis. There are, of course, other functions which the revelation model performs, and other norms for its employment; and to these we shall turn. In the meantime, I should like to enter a plea for the extension of the psychological model, in some respects at least to the divine nature, for how else can we properly speak about 'the mind of Christ' or indeed 'the will of God'?

[1] *The Gospel of the Incarnation*, SCM Press 1959, p. 91.
[2] See above, pp. 133f.

6

THE REVELATION MODEL

SYNOPSIS

In the Old Testament, the paradigm of the revelation model is triadic in form: *A reveals B to C.*

But each of the terms in this model has to be qualified:

A becomes A(x) where x draws attention to the fact that A bears a supernatural interpretation.

B becomes B(y) when y signifies some aspect, purpose, will of God (B).

C becomes C(Holy Spirit) obviously to draw attention to the revelatory function of the third person of the Trinity.

In the New Testament, we require two paradigmatic forms.

A(x) reveals B(A) to C(Holy Spirit).

B(A) reveals B(E) to C(Holy Spirit).

A = the man Jesus   B = God   B(A) = God in Christ.

B(E) = God as he is essentially in himself.

Examination of four cases of revelation model:
1. Fairweather.
2. Brunner.
3. Barth.
4. Dehn.

Difficulties of revelation model. 'Revelation is self-authenticating.' Revelation as a formal structure, deriving content from other Categories. Revelation is a second-order model.

Important consequences follow in christology from the combination of revelation model with (*a*) the psychological model and (*b*) the two-nature model.

Discussion of kerygmatic value of the revelation model.

The Revelation Model

HERE, UNTIL a year ago, we would have been approaching the totally, universally accepted mid-twentieth century christological model. Barth might disagree with Brunner on the extent and nature of the effect of the fall of man upon the image of God in man, or about the range of revelation. Barth and Bultmann might disagree about how history and myth are related to one another in the Gospel; Pittenger might criticize the christology of the kenoticists; but all to a man they would rally to a single standard when the question of whether the term 'revelation' is the right one to apply to Jesus Christ. Revelation is what Christianity is about. Revelation is the totality of the faith. To deny revelation is to be not a heretic, but a blasphemer. Suddenly, publicly a year ago in the midst of this universal, ecumenical chorus, there was heard a strident, discordant note—though perhaps the word 'note' is not appropriately applied to such a lengthy, detailed and sustained analysis of the case for revelation. I refer to F. Gerald Downing's *Has Christianity a Revelation?*[1] The publication of that book will make it unnecessary for me to say some of the things that I meant to say. It will affect some of the things I shall have to say, because I shall be obliged to orient myself by its position. But since Mr Downing's purpose was rather different from mine in this present exercise, I expect to say things to which he has not given his attention.

A matter which we have not so far examined is that of how the human mind arrives at the models with which it operates in extending its christological structures. By this time it must be clear that they are not given by the Holy Spirit to the mind of man: they bear too many marks of human ratiocination for us to accept such a naive suggestion. Downing does certainly show that those who think to absolutize the revelation model by claiming that it is part of the scriptural witness to Christ are guilty either of false exegesis or of theological incompetence to

[1] SCM Press 1964.

understand what is involved in the revelation model. But it would be wrong to think that we have dismissed the revelation model by showing that it is not given in scripture in so many words. (Downing himself does not think so because, in addition to demonstrating the inadequacy of the biblical texts thought to validate revelation, he contributes a very thorough analysis of theological uses of the term.) Since, however, so many of our contemporaries regard this model as absolutely normative for all christology and theology we may perhaps best begin by out-lining the structure of this model.

The structure of the revelation model: the Old Testament

I should like to take as my starting-point an analysis of the revelation model which I worked out a number of years ago.[1] At that time I began by reviewing the biblical texts which in-cluded words that might be translated by the English word 'reveal', but my doubts about the validity of that procedure which I stated then have now been more than confirmed. The basic revelation model takes the form *A reveals B to C*, but this form requires to be qualified as we apply it separately to the Old Testament and to the New Testament.

When we try to make this model operate by giving Old Testa-ment values to the symbols, at first it appears that A and C are the variables and B is the constant. In order to derive a real revelation situation from the model, we give to A the value 'the drying up of the Red Sea' or 'the burning of the bush that was not consumed' or 'the firmament'; to B the value 'God', and to C the value 'Moses' or 'David'. The revelation situation then reads, 'The drying up of the Red Sea reveals God to Moses'; 'The burning of the bush that was not consumed reveals God to Moses'; 'The firmament reveals God to David the psalmist'. The revelation model is thus seen to entail a triadic relation, a three-term relation, the three relata being revealer, the re-vealed and the recipient of the revelation. If any one of the three is missing there is no revelation.

On examination the initial simplicity of our model will be found to have deceived us in respect of each of its constituent terms. The triadic character of the model remains as its funda-

[1] See *The Reformed Theological Review*, 1956, 1957.

mental structure, but the terms require to be carefully qualified. Let us look at each in turn.

Modification of A

A is that circumstance, thing, event in the world which reveals God to the believer. But in fact if it is to appear in the model at all it has, in being A, to be more than A. Take the simple case of the drying up of the Red Sea. We may describe this event (as many in 1940 similarly described the weather conditions surrounding the rescue of allied troops on the Dunkirk beaches) in terms of possible, though perhaps unusual, climatic conditions obtaining at that time in the sea between the great land masses of Africa and Arabia; conditions precisely created by immediately previous and long-term causes to which it could be related in terms of barometric pressures, air temperatures, wind velocities, and tides. But so long as the Red Sea event is related only to previous events in the space-time continuum, it can have no place in the revelation model. It has to point beyond itself, to have, as it were, a perpendicular as well as a horizontal reference, in order to appear within the model. The burning bush might be described as a trick of the sunlight, as some kind of optical illusion, or as a form of mirage, which could be precisely accounted for in terms of the laws of light and optics. But when the burning bush appears in the revelation model *A reveals B to C* it rejects the natural or naturalistic description as total, and it claims a character which may even conflict radically with that description.

Without the possibility of its pointing beyond itself, A could not appear as a member in the revelation model; at best it might demonstrate the validity of the laws of light or optics. The stars in their courses, in the same way, might be described naturalistically by reference to the laws of astrophysics; but when the firmament is said to declare the handiwork of God we have gone beyond that description of the stars, not eliminating it altogether, but incorporating it in a fuller interpretation which regards the stars as symbolic of an order operative in the ethical as well as in the natural sphere. In order to represent this fact in the revelation model, I propose to qualify A by x and to say that $A(x)$ *reveals B to C*, A(x) meaning that A in

addition to its natural description bears a supernatural interpretation which permits it to appear in the revelation model.

A very similar point has been variously made by two theologians widely separated in time and outlook, St Thomas
Aquinas and H. H. Farmer. St Thomas wrote:

> God is only known through his effects (*per suos effectus*) or
> through the things he has made (*per ea quae facta sunt*).[1]

The natural order was not for St Thomas exhaustively describable in terms of natural laws; it had the further character of
'being an effect', of pointing beyond itself to a reality upon
which it was dependent for its being and characteristics. In
other words for St Thomas the x in $A(x)$ means that A has the
further non-natural quality of 'being an effect of'. Here we see
rather readily why there should be so much disagreement between the theist and the non-theist over the validity of the
classical proofs of divine existence. The non-theist regards the
term appearing in the premise upon whose character the argument turns as being solely A; and he denies that it has the qualities which the theist uses in the construction of the arguments.
The theist, on the other hand, begins not from A but from $A(x)$
and he has no great difficulty in showing that if A is an effect,
then it must have a cause. This form of the argument is therefore not unjustly criticized for being simply the unwrapping of
a definition, the explication of a tautology. On such a reading,
of course, the proofs of divine existence are assumed to be derivative in the first instance from revelation situations, an assumption which is not entirely unwarranted as one discovers if he
tries to state whence the notion of the world as an effect could
have been derived.

In a quite different setting H. H. Farmer[2] speaks of the world
as 'God's symbol' and explains his view in terms similar to those
we have used:

> The triadic relationship of God, man and the world, involving
> that both man and his world should have significance for God,
> and a relative independence over against God as well as over
> against one another, involving also that man would know God

---

[1] *Summa Theologica*, I.2.ii; *Summa contra Gentiles*, I.12.
[2] *The World and God*, Nisbet 1939, pp. 68ff.

through the world yet not be separated from God by the world, is doubtless very mystifying for the reflective mind, especially when the religious man goes on to affirm that none the less all things live and move and have their being in God.

In fact if I might modify what Farmer says, the world is an incomplete symbol, in the sense that it is a symbol for a relationship whose nature is indicated but whose two, or three, terms are not stated. It is the incomplete character of the world as symbol which gives St Thomas' arguments such plausibility as they have and prevents them from being at least obvious tautologies. It is this incompleteness which is called the *contingentia mundi* and forms the basis of all metaphysical theories which deny that the world is self-explanatory.

Modification of B

By this time, we have become suspicious of the simplicity of the original model, *A reveals B to C*; and we cannot but pursue our suspicions. What is it that A(x) reveals to C? Since it is still the revelation in the Old Testament that we are discussing, we cannot say that it is God's essence that A(x) reveals. We are obliged to say that it is some purpose of God's, some aspect of his being or nature, some attitude of his to the behaviour of his people, some statement of God's, some reaction to events in the world, and so on. Thus, it might be God's anger with Sodom and Gomorrah, his resolute purpose to free Israel from the hand of the Egyptians, his will for the way in which men and women should live in society and how they should honour him as their creator and saviour, or his continuing willingness to forgive them their sins. So once again we modify the model, to say that *A(x) reveals B(y) to C*. B(y) then appears as the completion of the incomplete symbol A(x). If the world is symbol, God is that of which, or he of whom, it is symbolic. If the Red Sea in its odd behaviour is symbolic, we know now that it points beyond itself to the reality of God's intention to save his people Israel.

Modification of C

The modification of the third term in our revelation model is one which has proved to be of tremendous importance in the history of theology. The modification arises for the following reason. While C is the end-term in the process covered by the revelation model, he is not a passive recipient. Indeed, he may be active in two ways. On the one hand, he may strenuously resist the whole endeavour of God to reveal himself to him, and the process may be in danger of frustration and defeat at this very point, because of man's sin. On the other hand, while he may bring all the power and insight, of which he is capable, to the revelation situation, the appropriation of it is something well beyond his capacities. So the doctrine of the Holy Spirit, or of the indwelling grace of God, has begun to appear in the Old Testament, though it is given its fullest and clearest expression in the New Testament. We qualify the C in our model with the terms Holy Spirit to give C(Holy Spirit). I make this modification without any commitment on how the believer and the Holy Spirit are related to one another in this process, beyond the rejection of Pelagianism. We have then for the Old Testament what I shall call model one: *A(x) reveals B(y) to C(Holy Spirit)*.

Structure of the revelation model: the New Testament

We may make our first attempt to form a revelation model for the revelation of God in Jesus Christ recorded in the New Testament, by adopting and adapting that which we evolved for the Old Testament in the following way. *A(x) reveals B(A) to C(Holy Spirit)*. A(x) has the kind of connotation which it had before. A is the ordinary human life of the man Jesus, as it would appear to the people of his day regardless of whether they believed in him or not, his life as it would be written down by a modern scientific historian. The x draws attention to the fact that this life points beyond itself to a reality which is not inspectable by empirical reason, but is known only to faith. Once again A(x) is an incomplete symbol; so far the non-material reality to which A points and of whose significance it is the bearer, has not been specified.

It will be observed that we have altered the second relatum in the model from B(y) to B(A), and the purpose of the alteration is twofold. On the one hand, we want to do justice to the claim made by theologians who use this model that in Jesus

God reveals not just one of his attributes, or some aspect of his nature or even his whole purpose for mankind, but his very self; and so the B is retained in the model and the y because it denoted only an attitude, reaction, purpose or attribute of God, is eliminated. At the same time, on the other hand, it is obvious that in Jesus the naked glory of God's majesty is not beheld, and that we have to do, in the first instance, with the Word *made flesh*, God in Christ Jesus, God as a man among men. For this circumstance, I would use the symbol B(A), God in Jesus Christ. At this stage I am making no suggestions about how the B and the A are related to one another. Perhaps some form of kenoticism may readily appear to enable us to say that B(A) represents the divine nature, as it is accommodated to the limitations and privations of human existence. But there is no obligation on us to say how B and A are related beyond insisting that they are compresent.

The final term in the model C(Holy Spirit) remains it would seem unchanged, though two comments might be made. First, the Holy Spirit now directs the believer specifically to Jesus Christ in revealing God, so that his work is limited and defined by the finished work of Christ. Secondly, it is not possible completely to tidy up terminology; for the actual work of consummating the revelation is at one point in the New Testament assigned not to the Holy Spirit but to the Father. At Matt. 16.17, after Peter has confessed Christ to be the Son of the living God, Jesus says that it is not flesh and blood that has revealed this fact to him, but 'my Father which is in heaven'. So then we have as model two, *A(x) reveals B(A) to C(Holy Spirit)*.

We have not quite done full justice to all that is said about the revelation of God in Jesus Christ, and particularly to the fact that God as he is known in Jesus Christ, our B(A), is substantially or even consubstantially the same as God is from eternity to eternity. This fact, it will be recalled, was the basis for Barth's rejection of the *consilium arcanum* of Calvinism, the decree according to which God predestines apart from Christ, that certain people, the reprobate, from the mass of sinners, will be damned to hell, while others, the elect, are saved in Jesus Christ. It was unthinkable that God should hold back some aspect of his nature, some secret purpose, when he was making his mind and purpose known to all mankind in Jesus Christ. In having to do with God as he is in Christ, we have to do with God as he is in and for himself. It seems necessary, therefore, to add model three to the other two, and to say: *B(A) reveals B(E) to C(Holy Ghost)*. To give values to the terms in the model: The God-man, Jesus Christ, reveals God as he essentially is to the believer inspired by the Holy Spirit. Model three also entails that the believer who wishes to know more about God as he is in himself will be obliged to return constantly to the God-man, Jesus Christ. In this sense, the revelation in Jesus Christ is exclusive. Model three is too the point of departure for the search which has constituted traditional christology as we know it, the search for a formula to describe the relation of the B in B(A) to the B in B(E); a search, also, which has led to the explication of the doctrine of the Trinity when the relation of the Holy Spirit to the other two terms in the model has been raised.

Biblical texts about revelation

It is necessary before leaving this discussion of the revelation models to say something of their relation to the biblical texts which are normally offered in support of a doctrine, or a concept, of revelation. It has to be admitted at once that the triadic character of model one is not borne out by the majority of Old Testament texts. A wide range of Hebrew words has been called in as evidence, notably, *galah*, reveal; *ra'ah*, see; *'amar*, say; *saphar*, tell; *yada'*, know; and their several Hebrew modifications; but Downing's list[1] of the ways the term 'reveal' is used in talk about God—of theophanies, of 'open' activities of God, of God's communication of secret information about the future, or of God's opening of men's eyes to see a vision—accords more with a dyadic view of revelation than with a triadic. There are two texts—in Ps. 97.6, 'The heavens declare his righteousness, and all the people have seen his glory', and in Ps. 19.1, 'The heavens declare the glory of God and the firmament shews his handiwork' (to the psalmist)—which with slight additions could be cast in the triadic mould, as indeed we did with one of them above. But I am rather inclined to think that

[1] *Has Christianity a Revelation?*, pp. 21ff.

Downing's exegesis is more accurate[1] when he says that these are texts not about revelation at all, but about praise—the praise offered to God by the heavens and the whole firmament. 'Praise is for the sake of praise and not for edification.' Nor is the case much better when we come to the New Testament. The most common reference of the term *apokalyptein* is consistently eschatological; while the only text (Luke 10.22 = Matt. 11.27) which bears the clearly triadic character of our analysis is either open to such a variety of possible interpretations, or so much a *hapax legomenon*, as not to be a sufficiently reliable basis for a total theory of revelation, or for anything approaching our models two and three. It has always seemed to me to be a strange anomaly that the concept of revelation which has become such a popular term in modern theology should have so little biblical basis for its employment. The anomaly is all the more serious when it is remembered that strong claims are made by revelation theologies to be also biblically based. I have no desire to labour those points now. But I would like to anticipate any premature dismissal of the revelation model on the score of its being non-biblical. It is a necessary part of theological construction that it employs in the deployment of its material many concepts which are not biblical. The Chalcedonian definition would have won no recognition whatsoever had it been required to pass the test of strict biblical literal documentation. The justification for any model will lie in the success it has in yielding insight into the basic christological material. Downing[2] argues at considerable length that the revelation model fails that test as well, but before agreeing with his sombre judgment I should like, with the help of the above analysis of the revelation model, to explore some of the variations in its use even by theologians who are in close sympathy with one another.

Forms of the revelation model: A. A. M. Fairweather

The first example I take is to be found in A. A. M. Fairweather's *The Word as Truth*.[3] This book is a comparative study of the epistemology of St Thomas Aquinas and Karl Barth. I am not concerned with the general themes of the book so much as with three statements made on p. 7, because they provide an

---

[1] *Op. cit.*, p. 24.   [2] *Op. cit.*   [3] Lutterworth Press 1939, p. 7.

interesting contrast with the more modern position, and show how very dissimilar statements can be made with the use of the revelation model. Sentence one: 'God cannot reveal himself by his pure presence.' Sentence two: 'Revelation cannot therefore direct our understanding to God himself and quite alone.' Sentence three: 'God manifests himself only in and through what is not himself, as God in continuity with some reality which we can perceive.' The noteworthy points in this position are as follows. We have to begin with in sentence one a denial of the dyadic character of the revelation situation. Revelation is not a theophany, the naked appearance of God before us, and in sentence three the recognition of the triadic character of the model: God, the reality through which God reveals himself, and ourselves as the recipients of revelation. This is stated in a rather interesting way, however, by saying that it is through what is *not* himself that God reveals himself. This view is a close reflection of St Thomas' theory that God is known through his effects, through what he has made. Revelation, any revelation, therefore entails some kind of diminution of God's stature, some form of *kenosis*, some assumption that God achieves what appears *a priori* to be quite impossible, that he should be known in and through what is less than he is. In fact we have now a possible alternative form of the revelation model—*Non-B reveals B to C*.

Next the quotations from Fairweather draw our attention to a fact which we have so far ignored, namely, that the revelation model has perhaps a still more complex internal structure than we have been prepared to admit. A paradigm revelation sentence would be: God reveals himself through history (or nature or Jesus Christ) to believers; or in model form: *B reveals B through A to C*. This form would, I agree, be theoretically the more correct but in the Old Testament passages we mentioned, 'The heavens declare the glory of God' (to the psalmist), and in the common account of the New Testament situation, 'Jesus Christ is the revelation of (i.e. reveals) God to the disciples', there lies justification for taking the direct non-reflexive form of the model.

Further, by saying that God manifests himself as God 'in continuity with some reality which we can see', Fairweather draws attention to the difficulty of describing the relation between God and the reality through which he is revealed. It is obviously not an analytic relation, so that by examining this reality we could discover God within it. Revelation does not imply pantheism, or even panentheism. Nor is it a relationship in which God so transforms that with which he is in continuity in revelation that it is deified. Human nature is not changed into divine when the Word is made flesh. Nevertheless whatever God has touched in revelation carries for evermore that stamp. This is the truth in sacramentalism.

I wonder, finally, however, whether Fairweather wishes to accept all the implications of his second statement, namely that, 'Revelation cannot therefore direct our understanding to God himself and quite alone'. He may simply be reiterating the point that in revelation it is not God out of all relation to reality that we know. But it is perhaps important to draw attention to the fact that in spite of the presence of the reality which is not God, we nevertheless do know God in himself. It is not simply a case of knowing $God + p$, $God + q$ and $God + r$, but that despite this conjunction the identity of God is established and his purpose and will for us identified. God is in a sense, therefore, isolated; our understanding is ultimately directed to himself and to him alone. I should add that Fairweather does later go on to mention the immediacy of knowledge of God which takes place 'in, with and under' the various media of revelation. But the quotation examined draws attention to a possible false extension of this kind of theory.

Emil Brunner: The Mediator

The variation in the use of the revelation model to which I previously referred could not perhaps be more dramatically illustrated than by contrasting Fairweather's sentence, 'God manifests himself in and through what is not himself' with the opening sentence of the English translation of Emil Brunner's *The Mediator*[1]: 'Through God alone can God be known.' I find this statement exceedingly ambiguous. It might mean at least three things.

First, it may be an emphatic way of affirming that in our knowledge of God, it is God who takes the initiative. It is only

---

[1] Lutterworth Press 1934, p. 21.

because God has decided to be known, only because he has chosen to emerge from the depth of his hidden-ness that men know who he is and what his purpose is for them. I think that this interpretation gives us the clue to the wide prevalence of the notion of revelation in modern theology. It is an attempt to do justice to the way in which God breaks into our lives. We find him because he has first found us. Religion, in other words, is revelation and not discovery. Brunner makes the big break with those who share many of his other views, when he adds that, 'this is a principle common to all religion'. It is no longer possible to argue that the distinctive thing about Christianity is that it has revelation. What distinguishes it is the content of its revelation. It is not difficult to see how Brunner reaches his conclusions about natural theology from this premise. In all religion, in all revelation, God is taking the initiative with men.

Secondly, another point could be being made by Brunner, and perhaps is, namely, that sin has so laid hold of man that he is unable of himself to see God, in nature, in history or in Jesus Christ. God has to break this power which binds man; he has to open man's eyes and only then does revelation take place. On this reading, Brunner is drawing attention to the presence of the Holy Spirit on the side of C, the believer, in our revelation models in all forms. God in his Spirit crosses over to our side to ensure that the purposes of his self-revelation will not finally be frustrated.

Let us look at a third possibility, for it is this that Brunner, I think, really intends, namely, that in the revelation situation, since God is God, he cannot reveal himself through anything less than himself. He must reveal himself through himself. But let us now see what this view entails when applied to our revelation models. Model one, $A(x)$ *reveals* $B(y)$ *to* $C(Holy Spirit)$, is directly controverted by Brunner's statement; for on this model God is not the medium through which revelation takes place: God is the subject of revelation. Here Fairweather is correct: God is known through what is other than God. Model two is the application, with slight modification, of model one to the revelation in Jesus Christ. $A(x)$ *reveals* $B(A)$ *to* $C(Holy Spirit)$. Once again if Brunner's account is correct, God is made the medium rather than the subject of revelation. It is only when we come to model three that we do see a possible interpretation of Brunner's sentence which is acceptable. Model three was: $B(A)$ *reveals* $B(E)$ *to* $C(Holy\ Spirit)$. God as he is in Jesus Christ reveals God as he is in himself to the faithful believer through the inspiration of the Holy Spirit. In this case God could be said to be both the medium and the subject of revelation, though we have to remind ourselves that model three presupposed model two for its right understanding and development. What is certainly clear is that we cannot give a simple yes or no to Brunner's formula, nor does it make any real sense if we take it by itself.

Karl Barth on the subject of revelation

It is impossible in any treatment of the revelation model either to omit reference to Karl Barth or yet to do anything approaching justice to all that he says. Out of the many matters that might be mentioned I wish to select only three. The first is a statement almost identical with that quotation from Brunner which we have just been examining, but he makes it in a much more sophisticated way. In *The Doctrine of the Word of God*[1] he sets down the revelation situation in three sentences: Sentence one: 'God reveals Himself.' Sentence two: 'God reveals Himself through Himself.' Sentence three: 'God reveals *Himself*.' He is making three emphases in this order. In the act of revelation, it is God who takes the initiative, and the whole event has its roots in divine grace. He executes the revelation not through any medium less than himself, but through his *alter ego*. Finally, as a result of this process, he genuinely reveals himself to man, and not just a part of himself or some aspect of his being. In this Barth effectively reduces revelation to our model three: $B(A)$ *reveals* $B(E)$ *to* $C(Holy\ Ghost)$. This concentration upon the revelation of God through God, of $B(E)$ through $B(A)$, has led to that neglect of the second model, which bases the revelation event upon a historical person, Jesus of Nazareth, which we already observed to be a residual element of Kierkegaardian scepticism in Barth.[2]

Barth later makes an interesting comment upon the content of the revelation whose divine source and character is thus so

[1] (ET), 1936, p. 340.   [2] *Op. cit.*, pp. 351, 353.

firmly guaranteed. He says that the revelation attested by scripture is that 'God reveals Himself as the Lord', and that this is an analytical judgment. Leaving till our next paragraph the use that Barth makes of this unusual summary of the content of biblical revelation, we may relate his account of it as an analytical judgment to our revelation models. Barth has his own account to give of what he means by an analytical judgment. Normally an analytical judgment is taken to be one in which analysis of the subject reveals the predicate to be contained by definition within it. Barth gives a slightly more difficult account of the matter. The revelation judgment is analytical 'because the distinction between form and content cannot be applied' to it. What I think he means is that whereas in other circumstances an alteration of form would entail an alteration of content, or the possibility of alteration of content, in the case of revelation, the fact that God exists in the form of a man does not entail any change in his nature from what he had been from all eternity. The content remains identical in the two situations; otherwise we would be obliged to deny the occurrence of revelation. The point is a good one to make, but whether it is altogether safe to make it in this way is another matter. The impression Barth may just create is that by examination of B(A), God as he is present in Jesus Christ, one automatically recognizes that B(A) is equivalent to B(E). If we know what the term 'triangle' means, we know by analysis of this concept that a three-sided rectilinear figure has three angles. But in our model three the transition from B(A) to B(E)—from the recognition that God is present in Jesus Christ (as he is present in John the Baptist) to the assertions that the fulness of God dwells bodily in Christ and the God thus present is co-essential with the Eternal God—is itself the subject of revelation and not the result of analysis.

We turn now to a second matter Barth raises in relation to revelation. One of the main uses, of course, made by Karl Barth in *The Doctrine of the Word of God* of the revelation model is that by summarizing the content of biblical revelation in the 'analytical judgment' mentioned above, he provides a basis for the doctrine of the Trinity, what he calls 'the root of the doctrine'. The interpretation he gives of how the doctrine of the Trinity is related to Scripture, through a whole series of media—the concept of revelation ('We come to the doctrine of the Trinity by no other way than by an analysis of the concept of revelation'[1]), the summary proposition about revelation, and even the constituent terms in revelation, Revealer, Revelation, Revealedness—is one of the most elaborate exercises in modern hermeneutics that I have ever encountered. But Barth is saying in effect that there is a threefoldness in the revelation situation, the triadic structure which we embodied in our revelation models, which qualifies it to provide a basis for the doctrine of the Trinity. Against the suggestion that we could arrive at the threefoldness of God simply by juggling with the logical structure of the notion of revelation, he replies very firmly that this sort of doctrinal extension of the revelation can only be carried out with the Christian model of revelation and with no other. What Barth does not indicate clearly enough is the quite unhistorical character of the exposition he gives of the root of the doctrine. Revelation considerations in no way affected the course of the great trinitarian controversies in the third and fourth centuries; and even now would carry conviction only to those who were prepared to accept Barth's rather esoteric approach to the subject. What Barth does make clear is the fact that the doctrine of the Trinity is not in the Bible, that it involves 'availing itself of other concepts than those contained in the (biblical) text before it'.[2] Once this character of the doctrine is recognized, then there is never any question of 'reading it off' from a biblical script. It is a very complex process of interpreting, checking, analysing and expounding that finally yields us the doctrine; and it is exceedingly difficult, at some stage in that process not to yield to the argument from tradition.

Thirdly, in *The Doctrine of the Word of God* Barth has, we have just seen, operated a fairly conventional model of revelation. The source of the revelation is the Revealer. The medium through which he is revealed is the Revelation. The result for the person apprehending the whole event is the Revealedness of the Revealer. All rather wordy, but basically simple. B reveals A to produce revealedness for C. On this model, the medium of Revelation is the whole event of Jesus Christ, the

[1] *Op. cit.*, p. 358. [2] *Op. cit.*, p. 354.

incarnation in its composite totality. There appears, however, somewhat later in Barth's writing a model with a rather different internal structure. The modification is, I believe, of major importance for the understanding of how the revelation model is tending to be used today by Barth's followers. The explicit quotations giving this revised model are not extensive. What I would claim is that if we do use this revised model we make much more sense of Barth's more recent writings than we do by adhering to the early model. Within the framework of very strong assertions that no dualistic thinking must be allowed to divide the human from the divine, Barth says[1] quite clearly that 'the divine essence (nature) expresses and reveals itself wholly in the sphere of the human nature'. Also,[2] 'the saving act of God takes place in the man Jesus of Nazareth. The power and authority of God are revealed by him and to him, in his words and in his actions.' These quotations are definitely not against the run of play. Three times on earlier pages[3] Barth has spoken about the human essence of Jesus Christ being the *organ* of the nature or work of the Son as the Mediator, a judgment curiously reminiscent of the famous sentence attributed to Nestorius, 'Mary bore a man who was the organ of Godhead.'

What are we to make of this revision of the revelation model? Barth does seem to be saying quite definitely that the revelation which takes place in Jesus Christ takes place through the human nature. We seem to have reverted to Fairweather's position: God is revealed through what is not God. The charge of Nestorianism cannot quite be made to stick. It would if Barth were saying that in Jesus Christ there are two complete persons present in exactly the same way at the same time. He is saying something rather different, and much more subtle, namely, that the human nature is there in the ordinary empirical and inspectible way, but that the divine nature is 'there' only as it reveals itself through the human nature. It is 'there', we might say, revelationally, or if words meant what they said, apocalyptically. On this reading the relation between the two natures is to be understood not in terms of compresence or logical *enhypostasia*, or yet of *communicatio idiomatum*, but in terms of this quite peculiar

---

[1] *Church Dogmatics* (ET) IV/2, 1958. Cf. II/1, pp. 16f.   [2] *Op. cit.*, p. 99.
[3] Namely pp. 96ff.

and unique relation of revelation. If we were to accept such a view, we might then be able on the one hand, to go to the extreme with the kenoticists—and in fact Barth begins to approach that extreme in the volume referred to[1]; and yet, on the other hand, to affirm to the full the deity of the divine nature with its complete attributes all revelationally present in Jesus Christ. We have now effectively reached the position detected in H. R. Mackintosh.[2] To revert to our models: Barth on this reading has telescoped models two and three to give *A(x) reveals B(E) to C(Holy Spirit)*. It is the relation of revelation which constitutes the situation, binds it in a unity and justifies Barth's insistence that there is no dualistic thinking here. My own feeling is that if the revelation model is to be made to work in our time it has to take this form, and not the form which Brunner and the earlier Barth had favoured.

Hidden-ness and revelation: Gunther Dehn

This presentation of the revelation model facilitates the inclusion in our talk about the revelation of God of some very mystifying statements about the hidden-ness of God in his revelation. If God can be known through God alone, then there can be no room for hidden-ness. The medium must be as clear as the *revelation*. It is when we introduce what is not God and affirm that God is known through what is not God that we lay the foundation for a whole range of statements about God's concealment, statements which have a long history in Lutheran theology, and which are part of Barth's standard talk about revelation. A typical example is to be found in Gunther Dehn[3]:

> God is concealed even in his revelation . . . even among Christians there is a continual desire to get into contact with God directly in his revelation. . . . But God resists this desire by remaining always, even in his revelation, the hidden God . . . God becomes man . . . God's activity is interwoven with the events of human history (and in it) is not directly distinguishable from the history of mankind.

Indeed so effective is this process, that God does indeed conceal himself at the very point of revelation. I agree that some of

---

[1] IV/2, e.g. pp. 484ff.   [2] See above, pp. 133f.
[3] *Man and Revelation*, Hodder and Stoughton 1936, pp. 65f.

this kind of talk comes very close to being nonsense, and that it forms a very easy point of departure for all who want to take the leap. But if there is any sense in it, it lies here, in its indication, perhaps a little sensationally, that God reveals himself through what is not God, a man who is carpenter, whom we have known since childhood and talked to, who is maybe a little bit odd, but such a fine fellow that we look upon him as one of ourselves. If revelation had been written all over this man, if he had come with the unmistakable mark of the divine upon him, if there had been no concealment, then he would have been accepted at least by those who were supremely responsible for his death. The Pharisees, however we dislike them now, however we pillory them, were not God-haters. Nor had they given up looking for the Messiah. If they had been given a sign, one tiny sign, they would have accepted. But no. He was concealed. There Dehn is correct. There too is the case for saying that the revelation comes through what is not God, the other-than-God which so often effectively conceals it.

Difficulties for the revelation model

I should like next to examine the role which the revelation model may fulfil in modern christology and the status which is to be accorded to it, together with some of the problems which it creates and of which its more ardent supporters are curiously imperceptive. Let us look to begin with at some of the quite basic difficulties which Gerald Downing raises.[1] I shall set aside the fundamental problem of biblical foundations for the term— not because it is unimportant, for it seems to me to point to a quite radical revision of the way in which many so-called biblical theologians interpret their task—and instead concentrate on some of the more strictly systematic issues. For example, there is a whole series of difficulties which Downing encounters in the many accepted phrases about revelation. The term 'revelation' is associated with unveiling, with making clear something that is already hidden. But when we apply this term to Jesus the result is not exactly what we want—for all that might be meant is that God appears as Jesus; or to adopt the language of D. D. Evans, we 'look on' Jesus as God. But this usage does

[1] *Has Christianity a Revelation?*

not do justice to what happens in me and to me when Jesus reveals God to me. The notion of finality when applied to revelation creates trouble, for revelation is essentially an open-ended process. It is something that happens and must go on happening so long as men and women find God revealed to them in Jesus Christ. The here-and-now character of revelation prevents us from calling it once-for-all, except in some paltry sense such as that Jesus Christ was seen only at a certain period in human history and then 'once-for-all' time. Downing makes a brief reference[1] to a sentence about revelation which Barth has introduced into modern theology, namely, that 'revelation is self-authenticating'. Though he does not treat the view with the fulness it deserves, he does put his finger upon the basic problem which it must face, that of explaining the differences between allegedly 'self-authenticating' experiences of the self-same God. As he had just said 'consistent solipsism is impregnable', nor, may we add, does the assertion of the objectivity of a self-authenticating experience logically imply the objectivity of the entire character of the subject claiming self-authentication.

What is revealed?

In the end of the day, perhaps Downing might be said to be rejecting the concept of revelation simply because it is not borne out by the evidence.

> God's love may well be too profound for us ever to understand. But it is not traditional teaching to suggest that it is self-contradictory. If any 'mystery' is 'revealed' to present-day Christians with their kaleidoscopic beliefs, it is a mystery of diversity, and that by definition is not 'God'. The traditional image of the 'mystery of God' is an ocean too deep to plumb; but the total course of Christian theology makes it look like a maze so complex that everyone gets lost in his own way. If there is a 'revealed mystery', it is this that is 'revealed'. . . . The theologian is using a word that normally describes 'making clear' to mean 'leave unclear'.[2]

There is a certain tang to this sort of criticism, and it may even seem to have an iconoclastic quality. But it is difficult to resist

---

[1] *Op. cit.*, pp. 224f.   [2] *Op. cit.*, p. 229.

the conclusion that it is largely justified by the sharp conflict that exists upon so many fronts in contemporary theology, and by the bitterness of so many of these conflicts with its denial of the love that lies at the heart of the Christian faith. Downing sums up his scepticism concerning revelation as the clue to Christianity by the quite outspoken questioning of the whole idea that God intended 'to reveal himself' in Jesus Christ. He may do so—our Christian hope is that he will—in the end-time; and what he has done in Jesus Christ will prepare us to know as we are known—then. But 'a "revelation" of what cannot now be seen is not a "revelation" '.[1] The great contribution of Downing's book, despite critics, is that it points us in the direction where we shall find more effective models to describe Jesus Christ, and models that are also much more biblical. These are the models of redemption and salvation. These models, as we shall see later, cannot adequately be sustained by the revelation model.

Performatives parasitic

Before leaving the summary of some of Downing's position, I may perhaps mention two points that merit further consideration. The first is that there are certain circumstances which make the extension of the 'performative' analysis of language to religious language not entirely valid, for this reason. If we take a typical performative statement—such as the Queen might make, 'I hereby appoint you High Commissioner to India'—we can see that this statement is not a description of anything but the actual execution of an appointment. What must, however, be noted is that it occurs within a context which may have to be described if someone says that he does not know who the Queen is, or why she should be making an appointment to an office carried out six thousand miles away, or what a High Commissioner is. In other words, a performative statement is parasitic. For this reason we can never resolve religious statements altogether into 'performatives'. By their very nature as 'performatives' they entail for their understanding what we might call 'host' statements, some at least of which must be descriptive. The linguistic analysis of religious statements can-

[1] *Op. cit.*, p. 238.

not finally, therefore, replace the ontological enquiry concerning the descriptive account of the contextual framework of the performatives.

The second consideration that ought to be kept in mind in trying to make an assessment of Downing's rather searching analysis is that while it is true that the word 'revelation' strictly relates to the process of making known what was previously unknown, or unveiling what was previously hidden, in most recent theology it has come to be used synonymously even with the very term which Downing proposes as an alternative to revelation talk—salvation, or with reconciliation and redemption. In one sense this fact lends still greater weight to Downing's criticism; for if it does not make much sense to say that the revelation remains hidden it makes perhaps even less sense to say that some men are redeemed and are not aware of it or that they are partially redeemed. It is significant that in Barth as the *Church Dogmatics* theme unfolds itself, it is the fact of reconciliation in Christ which increasingly comes to take the strain of the argument, while the idea of revelation to some extent recedes. It is not without interest and relevance to Downing's analysis that the term 'revelation' has at many hands come virtually to lose all connotative sense and to operate solely as a denotative term. The result is one of the clumsiest redundancies or at best periphrases of modern christology, the phrase 'the revelation of God in Jesus Christ', which is used so frequently and unthinkingly that it means no more than the name 'Jesus Christ'. I am not forgetting that the name 'Jesus Christ' was for primitive Christians perhaps chiefly for Jewish Christians, itself a connotative phrase; but in the gentile world as in the modern world it became almost solely denotative. When it has reached that stage it is no longer a christological model.

Revelation and redemption: which is more ultimate?

We have observed how Downing wishes to substitute the soteriological for the revelation model, and how Barth shifts the emphasis from revelation to reconciliation. Both of these moves are, I am convinced, due primarily to the facts that the revelation model fails to sustain an adequate analysis of the death of Jesus Christ. Let us take a basic soteriological proposition: 'The death of Christ reveals the love of God to sinners.' This proposition may be integrated in the context of either of two quite different theories about the significance of the death of Christ.

On the one hand, we may say that the attitude of God to sinners has been solely and consistently one of love towards them. God has tried many methods under the old covenant to help them to understand this attitude of his to them. All had failed, so in the end he sent his own son to live among men and to die self-sacrificially, as a supreme illustration of God's love. Through Christ's death, no change was effected in God's relation to man: no obstacle between God and man was removed. In a sense nothing happened objectively. A very compelling illustration was offered.

On the other hand, a fairly definite attempt may be made to take up where the previous theory left off, to agree that indeed the death of Christ supremely reveals the love of God but it does so for a very definite reason. Between the sinner and God there stands the mass of human guilt which is an offence to God. Whereas God loves the sinner, this mass of guilt must be removed before that love can express itself in God's acceptance of man. God in Jesus Christ accepts the responsibility for this guilt and Christ bears in his body the pain and suffering for this guilt. In Christ, man the sinner, his sins forgiven, is acceptable to God. It is through these happenings, these objective events, that the love of God is illustrated or revealed.

It seems to me intolerable that such a range of soteriological variation should be comprehended within one phrase. It has certainly enabled those who have been unwilling to reject openly so-called 'objective' theories of atonement to employ language which was sufficiently ambiguous to conceal their allegiance. In a word then, the revelation model fails to extend into a sufficiently unambiguous soteriological structure to justify its exclusive use in christology.

Revelation model a formal structure

Again, it is not always appreciated that the revelation model is a strictly formal structure. It states that a certain formal relationship holds between B and A for C, but in itself it does not supply us with the content of B or A. For example, it has been argued that if it is true that Jesus Christ reveals God, then the deity of Christ is *ipso facto* demonstrated. But such a demonstration is not by itself valid. It requires to be supported by some concealed premise such as that of Brunner's which we have already examined at length, namely, through God alone can God be known. But without some such premise, and as has been said before it is not an easily supportable premise itself, no conclusions can be drawn from the revelation model by itself as to the content of B or A. Someone who wishes to argue that God may reveal himself through sunsets, or good music, or inspiring poetry, or some of the repetitive processes of nature, cannot be ruled out of court by any appeal to the revelation model *simpliciter*.

In fact, I would go farther and say that the controversy over natural and revealed theology is not a controversy over the revelation model at all, but over the values which the controversialists have endeavoured to import into the model. If you like, it is a quarrel about definitions. One side has said that revelation takes place only in Jesus Christ, or logically: no instances of revelation are other than instances of revelation in Jesus Christ; and the other side has said that revelation takes place in nature, in human moral effort, in human history, and so on. In terms of revelation, one side is as entitled to its definition as the other, for the revelation model *per se* may be given either set of values. One side can only gain the edge on the other, or at least seem to do so, when it substitutes for the revelation model one of its soteriological alternatives, and appealing to scripture, 'There is none other name under heaven . . . whereby we must be saved',[1] argues that even if there is revelation outside of Christ, it is 'sound and fury, signifying nothing'. This is not the place for any further elaboration of this moth-eaten controversy, but I do sometimes wonder whether it ought not to be settled by a simple appeal to fact. If there are indeed some people who can honestly say that God reveals himself to them apart from Jesus Christ, and if we are to presume that they know what revelation means (say, from their awareness of revelation in Jesus Christ), then I wonder whether it is valuable or indeed proper to prosecute the controversy against them.

[1] Acts 4.12.

Revelation model a second-order structure

Another way of stating the case that I am now making is to say that the revelation model is a second-order model which derives its meaning from other first-order models. A comparable case could be made for saying that the assertion of the deity or the divinity of Christ is a second-order statement about him. The first-order statement occurs in the form of the primitive Church's declaration that in Jesus Christ God has fulfilled all his promises to Israel. So effectively does the range of fulfilment surpass human capacity that it seems to have reached a degree of accomplishment that only God himself could achieve. The affirmation that 'Jesus is God' is then made. In some senses, the revelation model may quite justifiably be taken even as a third-order model, because it depends for its assertion, and for its content, both upon the first-order statements which the Bible makes concerning Jesus, and also for a whole group of theological statements which have found their way into creeds and confessions and stand in very close proximity to the biblical statements.

If this argument is correct then we have to say that Jesus Christ is the revelation of God because he is God incarnate; and we cannot say that the affirmation of the deity of Christ rests upon the prior declaration that he is the unique revelation of God. Revelation is not a theological conjuror's hat out of which we may draw the rabbits of the several doctrines of the Christian faith. The model of revelation is in fact dependent upon these models for its content and indeed for its form. For that reason, it becomes almost impossible to sustain Barth's positions, on which previously we kept an open mind, that we come to the doctrine of the Trinity by no other way than by the concept of revelation, or that the root of the doctrine is to be found in the revelation structure. In the hierarchy of doctrines the doctrine of the Trinity stands too high to be a derivative from a third-order doctrine such as that of revelation.

Revelation model and the psychological model

As a result of the previous aspects of the revelation model upon which we have been commenting—that it is formal and that it is a second- or even a third-order model—it tends to combine with other models (in addition as we noted above to giving way to them). This procedure is not always without its complications. Some of these we have noticed in connection with the two-nature model, and the psychological model. When the revelation model is combined with the two-nature model, one or other of two consequences follows.

Either, we have the rather curious circumstance that the divine nature is part of the situation which is the medium of revelation, or in some extremer forms of this view (Brunner and Barth, at times) that the divine nature is alone the medium of revelation and the human nature becomes an optional extra. I am not sure that we are not quite close to impermissible nonsense when we try to say that the divine nature can be both the medium and the subject of revelation (that is, without the additional apparatus of forms two and three of the revelation model). For *ex hypothesi* the medium of revelation is known directly, and if the medium and the subject of revelation are identical and thus known directly, there is no occasion for revelation.

Or, and this is, we said before, the only real alternative: the human nature *per se* is the medium of revelation (Barth on rare occasions) and it mediates the divine nature to us. This combination of the two-nature model with the revelation model would entail an almost entire re-writing of christological theory, and a very radical recasting of the two-model theory. Very little of the Aristotelianism which has been engrossed in modern enhypostatic theory would remain, as indeed would little of enhypostatic theory.

The combination of the revelation model with the psychological model would lead to a christological theory not unlike that which we have just mentioned. The chief difference would be that the human nature would be construed in more strictly psychological terms than would be available for Barth with his rather radical Kierkegaardian historical scepticism. This combination enables its expositors to give a more thoroughgoingly human account of Jesus' earthly life, the critics might say an even ebionite view, and relieves them of the recurring problem of explaining how a divine mind can be at the same time omniscient and ignorant, the same person omnipotent and weak. The essential and obvious humanity of many of Jesus' actions in the

New Testament has induced biblical theologians with a systematic bent to employ the revelation model to enable them to connect biblical accounts of these actions with standardized systematic theological interpretations of them. Here lies part-explanation of a practice to which Downing refers,[1] namely, the wide use of this model by biblical theologians despite the absence in the Bible of any general occurrence of the term to describe God's actions or purposes—that in the New Testament the revelation model provides a bridge between the biblical narratives and the systematic christological picture of Christ. But it is a procedure which is not entirely unexpected because of the formal character of the revelation model: by its nature it derives content from beyond itself.

Apologetic and kerygmatic value of the revelation model

To turn now to a quite different matter: the revelation model has often been thought to have great apologetic and kerygmatic value. The kerygmatic value, it is said, lies in the fact that in proclaiming God and his mercy and goodness, we are not under obligation to lay out the pathways which men and women must take to find God. He has already come to them. He has 'revealed' himself. He has appeared. The apologetic value of such a concept, it is said, is that it relieves us of all obligation to prove that God exists, or that he has done this or that, or that a certain interpretation is the only valid one to impose upon a given set of phenomena. This assessment of the value of the revelation model savours perhaps more of the safe seclusion of the pulpit than the rough-and-tumble of the common room, and one wonders how much longer it can continue to bewitch the insensitive and imperceptive.

Let us examine the situation more closely. The kerygmatic statement—that God has appeared among us—carries a *prima facie* persuasiveness only because the revelation thus asserted is taken to be dyadic, two-term, a direct face-to-face confrontation. But in fact this is not so. The situation kerygmatically described as God having revealed himself is that of a man called Jesus acting in this way and that and saying this and that. Immediately the stage is set for a very long argument about

[1] *Op. cit.*, p. 20 n. 1.

whether that claim to revelation is a fair interpretation of these words and actions. That argument does not concern me at present. But the fact that it can begin shows that the revelation situation is not dyadic but triadic (as we have all along contended) and that before the revelation model can be employed there must be at least some idea, some general notion accepted to which revelation is referred. Within the context of the Old and New Testaments this condition is fulfilled. The Jew can speak significantly of the God who was known to Abraham and Isaac *revealing* himself to the people of Israel in their sufferings in Babylon. The God who subsequently reveals himself is already identified by the people of Israel and acknowledged by them. In the New Testament Peter, had he been so moved, might have spoken of the God who had promised salvation to Israel revealing his salvation to men finally in Jesus Christ; and the proclamation of revelation would again be significant because God was known to his hearers.

But where there is no prior knowledge or acknowledgment of God, revelation propositions have no weight. If I say to an unbeliever 'God is revealed in Jesus Christ', this proposition means no more or no less than the term 'God' means. If God has no existence, the proposition cannot assist his revelation. Propositions asserting the revelation of God presuppose some prior knowledge of God if they are to have any significance. The assertion of God's being and God's revelation cannot significantly be made in one proposition. When we pursue this course, we begin to develop a sympathy which Protestant theology has not had for many decades now, for the proofs for divine existence. For among the many other things they may be trying to do there is this: they are endeavouring to establish a value for the term 'God' which might make a revelation proposition not just meaningful but actually possible. In short then, the revelation model has no real place in an apologetic situation where we are conversing with total unbelievers. It has a place in a kerygmatic utterance only where it is made in the context of some degree of accepted belief in God.

7

CONCLUSION

IT WILL be useful perhaps in conclusion to draw together one or two points which seem to be emerging from this examination of models and to make one general reflection upon the character of christological method and study. Concerning the models it must by this time be fairly obvious that it would be wrong to attach a compulsive character to any one of the models (or to try to offer some brand new model to lord it over those we have examined). Models seem to vary according to the circumstance in the christological situation which their exponents wish to emphasize or which they regard as specially important. It would be more difficult now than it was in our first chapter to argue for the specific given-ness of one model over any of the others. Someone might be tempted to call our bluff here and to argue that some pre-eminence should be given to the biblical models —Son of God, Son of Man, Logos or Messiah. But the very interesting fact is that there has not been in the history of christology proper—as distinct from biblical christological word-studies which one cannot regard as serious christology—any sustained attempt to elevate any one of those concepts into a thoroughgoing christological model. The Word of God model which we have not here considered has established itself and would merit detailed consideration on its own but it cannot be regarded as derived from the Logos concept, or yet as an extension of it into systematic christology. These biblical models had they been used in christological systematization might have had some claim to given-ness, some compulsive character. But their non-appearance in christology as models has eliminated even them from consideration. What has to be recognized, however, is that once we do adopt a model, it tends to become compulsive for us. It prescribes the kind of system we construct. It determines the method that we follow in such systematic construction. It sharpens and defines the presentation we give of the person of Jesus Christ.

Secondly, a self-critical examination of the models we employ in christology ought of itself to put us on our guard against too facile switching from one model to another. The most dangerous aspect of this kind of confusion is that we transfer from one model to the other categories, thought and inferential processes that are quite inappropriate to it. In some cases, this category switch may simply produce muddled thinking. In other cases it may actually inhibit the development of the second model. Such has been the fate of the psychological model. It has always felt obliged to stay within hailing distance of the two-nature model. If it has strayed beyond earshot, it has been forcibly retrieved and roundly chastised by the keepers of the two-nature model. But the two-nature model has itself suffered from the inhibition created by its bondage to Aristotelian logic and thus been prevented from expressing itself in other logical terms. The recognition of the relative independence of the models of one another is one condition of greater variety in christological expression.

Since it seems to be the case that no compulsive character can be attached to the models unless they are thought of as *given* to the theologian; since, too, the model seems to be a vehicle of varied christological expression and not uniform or standardised; the question might well be asked, Whence do models derive? The answer that commends itself to my judgment is that the creation of models is part of the function which imagination fulfils in theological activity. Theology has been singularly slow to allow imagination a place within its sacred precincts; and one ought not to be surprised if as a result a good deal of theology has been correspondingly unimaginative. This suspicion of imagination has had several sources. For example, it has been associated with phantasy-thought, with the creation of illusions, hallucinations or compensatory systems. It has been a medium of escape from the harshness of reality. It has, alternatively, either added to reality or presented a false picture of reality. At no time is it recognized as a medium of truth. For that reason it has acquired a moral stigma. There is no more complete condemnation of any story than to declare that it is 'pure imagination'. The scriptures have added their own toll of severe judgment on the term. 'For the imagination of man's heart is evil from his youth.'[1] There has been a fear, too, that if we allow imagination a place within the activity of theological construction we are giving formal recognition to the fact that man may discover truth for himself. That would be christological Pelagianism. Two replies may be made to this fear.

First, it is perfectly possible, if we wish, to safeguard the pneumatological proprieties, to say that in this process of imaginative construction man does receive the assistance and guidance of the Holy Spirit. The Holy Spirit would be thought of not as dictating a series of propositions which man could faithfully repeat, but as working creatively, as it were, from man's side. It is difficult, as we noticed before, to pursue any further description of the psychological process in which the Holy Spirit inspires the mind or will of man. *That* he does so is all that we are presently concerned to acknowledge, on this first reading of the situation.

The second and quite different reply to the fear that the acknowledgment of the presence of imagination in christological construction may concede too much to the ability of man to think for himself is to say that a good deal of the time in theology that is exactly what man does—he thinks for himself. There is a passage in *The Doctrine of the Word of God*[2] which comes surprisingly near to saying something similar:

> (Dogmatics) knows the light that is perfect in itself, that discovers all in a flash. But it knows it only in the prism of this act, which however radically or existentially it may be regarded, is a human act. . . . The creaturely form which God's revealing action comes to take in dogmatics is therefore not that of knowledge attained in a flash, which it would have to be to correspond to the divine gift, but a laborious advance from one partial human insight to another.

Barth here comes very close perhaps to wanting to have it both ways. Dogmatics 'knows the light that is perfect'—but the act of knowing is human and fallible. God's revealing act is the subject of dogmatics, but it is known in a process of advancing from one partial human insight to another. What Barth is say-

---

[1] Gen. 8.21d.   [2] p. 14.

ing, it seems to me, is simply this: God in his revelation—or as we would prefer to say, God in Jesus Christ—is the subject that dogmatics deals with; but it deals with this subject not by writing down a series of divinely communicated propositions, but by humanly and fallibly and painfully slowly thinking about them. Such thinking is a process involving perception and insight—both of which are, I should say, functions of imagination.

A good deal has been said in recent years about man having come of age, and I must confess that I cannot follow very much of it, for it seems to be a rather disguised way of saying that modern man is godless. It is the atheist's answer to 'Except ye become as little children'. But I can just see that in theology, we have in a sense to be ready to stand on our feet, to recognize that our theology, our christology, is *human* thinking about God, *human* thinking about Christ. There is an element of deceit in pretending that these are not our thoughts but God's thoughts, blasphemy, perhaps, more than deceit. The danger then is that we become so convinced that our thoughts are God's thoughts that we make a fair shape at reproducing the wrath of God against those who have the effrontery to disagree with us. Theology, christology, is none the worse for being humble—and none the less true for it, either.

It is for this reason that I should like to say a concluding word about christology, models and faith—two words in fact. On the one hand, if models are deliverances of imagination, we shall be a little reluctant to claim for them immediately the sanctions of faith. They do not come to us with the authority of Christ himself. They do not impose themselves upon us as the dazzling light of truth. They represent our partial insights, our slow advance from vantage-point to vantage-point. If we assign to them the sanctions of faith, very soon we find ourselves seeking to impose them upon our fellows; or we set up the machinery of the Inquisition or its Protestant forms of anathema, which are not without their painful consequences. Faith has Christ as its subject and its goal and nothing less.

On the other hand, it must be insisted that unless the models serve faith in the end of the day, neither will they justify themselves intellectually nor will they even survive. There is a theological schizophrenia as well as other sorts. It is the state of mind in which we cling with a return-to-the-womb desperation to the simple form in which we first found and expressed our faith; and at the same time practise all the sophistries of christological hair-splitting, existentialist elaboration and systematic proliferation. Schizophrenia is not a stable state of mind; and the tragedy is that when it finally resolves itself, both of its constituent elements are destroyed. Christological models, therefore, which are not derived from faith, will finally if they be true models find their place and their home in faith's worship of and prayer to its Saviour and Master.

INDEX OF SUBJECTS

Index of Proper Names

Unity, 74ff.
Universals, 105

Verification, 35

Word, the, 25, 67, 84, 124, 139f., 153, 157, 174; *see below, Logos*
Words, 103-6
Worship, 45, 49

INDEX OF PROPER NAMES

Abraham, 76, 171
Amos, 77
Anselm, St, 112
Apollinaris, 96f.
Aquinas, St Thomas, 148f., 153
Aristotle, 86ff., 95, 103
Austen, Jane, 137
Australia, 18
Ayer, A. J., 32

Baillie, D. M., 122, 124-6
Barth, K., 26, 36, 40, 74, 98f., 108-11, 122, 151, 157-61, 165, 169
Barton, B., 49
B.B.C., 41
Berkeley, Bishop, 102
Black, Max, 56
Bornkamm, G., 49, 115f., 126-8
Brunner, E., 49, 122, 155-7, 167, 169
Buber, M., 27, 31
Bulgakov, S., 125
Bultmann, R., 26, 40, 47, 106, 116f., 122, 127

Calvin, 26
Carrington, Archbishop, 46
Casserley, J. V. Langmead, 43
Collingwood, R. G., 28, 32, 42
Cuba, 35
Cyprus, 35
Cyril of Alexandria, 94

Davey, F. N., 86
David the Psalmist, 146
Dehn, G., 161f.
Dorner, J. A., 132
Downing, F. Gerald, 145f., 152f., 162-5, 170

Dunkirk, 146

Ebeling, G., 26
Ephraim of Antioch, 89, 99-101
Eutyches, 92
Evans, D. D., 162
Everest, 43

Fairweather, A. A. M., 153-5, 160
Farmer, H. H., 148
Father, 45, 85, 125, 139, 151
Forsyth, P. T., 132
Fosdick, H. E., 128f.
Frost, David, 41

Gess, 132
God, 22, 31, 36
image of, 110
God-man, 43, 134f.
Graham, Dr Billy, 41

Hastings, 136
Heidegger, J. H., 98
Heidegger, M., 28, 106
Heim, K., 131
Hendry, G. S., 143
Hippolytus, 89
Hodgson, L., 129, 136, 140
Hollaz, D., 98
Hoskyns, E., 86
Hume, D., 102

India, 164
Inquisition, 175
Isaac, 171

James, St, 78
John, St, 46, 69, 86